UNDERSTANDING SEPARATION

GREGORY K. RIGGEN

Other Books by This Author:

Understanding the Godhead

Understanding the New Birth

Calling on the Name of the Lord (an in-home Bible Study)

Do All Speak with Tongues? (an in-home Bible Study)

Lessons on Prayer (download only)

Bible Reading Made Easy (daily reading chart; free download)

Order from:

The Truth Church of Olathe, Kansas

http://www.olathetruth.com/resources

All Scripture quotations are from the King James Version of the Holy Bible, unless otherwise noted.

Copyright © 2025 Gregory K. Riggen
All rights reserved.
ISBN: 978-1-7330572-4-0

DEDICATION

This book is dedicated to the wonderful saints of God who "hunger and thirst after righteousness" and the great men of God who declare it unashamedly. I sincerely pray what is written here will help satisfy the longing of the laity and strengthen the hands of the ministry.

CONTENTS

	Acknowledgements	i
	Preface	1
1	The Premier Principles	7
2	Transformed, Not Conformed	17
3	Be Ye Separate	33
4	A Right Spirit	43
5	The Need for Standards	59
6	Lifting a Standard	77
7	Present Your Bodies	91
8	Guarding Your Tongue	115
9	Guarding Your Eyes	131
10	Guarding Against Immorality	145
11	Outward Adorning	161
12	Hair – the Long and Short of It	179
13	Psalms, Hymns, and Spiritual Songs	199
14	Grieve Not the Spirit	221
	Bibliography	241
	About the Author	249

ACKNOWLEDGMENTS

I would like to express my sincere appreciation to everyone who helped make this book a reality. First, it was Bishop Gary Howard's encouragement that became the catalyst for me to write. Second, my wife has spent untold hours reading, re-reading, editing, and working alongside me throughout this process. Also, Brother Jared Hilton (my Associate Pastor) has gone above and beyond the call of duty in helping me with this effort. I also appreciate the others who served as proofreaders and editors, including Pastor John Burgess, Pastor Joe Savala, Evangelist Tim Wodoslawsky, and my son-in-law, Major D.J. Uribe (USAF). Their input has been invaluable. Finally, I want to thank Sister Jasmine Olmos for the cover design. To each and every one of you, words are not adequate to convey my deep gratitude. The words, "Thank You!" do not seem sufficient. Just know that I am truly appreciative.

PREFACE
THE REASON FOR WRITING

For several years now, I have had people ask me to compile a book about Apostolic Doctrine. I have repeatedly shrugged off any such suggestions, as I recognize that (1) there are already many scholarly works available on every area of this truth, and (2) the way I teach doctrine is extremely simple and, accordingly, might be rejected by those expecting a more "scholarly" approach.

Several things happened that brought about a change of mind. First was the tremendous success we have been seeing in converting Trinitarian preachers on the continent of Africa. This volume would be extremely lengthy if I described in detail just how successful we have been, so I will give just a brief synopsis.

Beginning in 2013 and continuing until (and most likely long after) the printing of this book, God has enabled me to travel to several African countries and teach Apostolic Doctrine to thousands of Trinitarian ministers and their wives. We have seen God repeatedly open their eyes to subjects such as the oneness of God, baptism in Jesus' name, the necessity of the Holy Ghost, and separation from the world. They, in turn, go back to their congregations and teach what they have learned. As a result, they have baptized the majority (if not all) of the members of their congregations. We give God all glory because we acknowledge this to be a work of His Spirit, not the results of our talents,

Preface

abilities, or intellect. However, we also see that God has repeatedly used our simple, methodical presentation to accommodate this great revival.

The second thing that happened was that I suddenly received several invitations to teach doctrine in Apostolic churches here in the United States of America. Whenever I accepted the invitation, I made it a point to tell the host pastor and congregation that they should not expect profundities, as I do not try to "go deep" when teaching these truths. Instead, I try to present our message as simply as possible, making it understandable to virtually anyone with an open mind. What I have seen during these sessions has, quite honestly, amazed me. Over and over, good saints of God (some of whom have been, by their own testimony, "serving the Lord for many years") have come to thank me for helping them to get a better grasp of the truth and, in some cases, a revelation of truth for the very first time!

With these two factors already working together, the third and final factor came into play. While teaching at Tulsa Lighthouse Church in Tulsa, Oklahoma, Elder Gary Howard, the man I was privileged to call my pastor for over 20 years, asked me to write a book about our doctrine. My love and appreciation for Bishop Howard is deep. Any suggestions or requests from him carried much more weight with me than those of others. When he brought it up, I knew it was time. Within days, I sat down to begin this project.

As I worked, though, I soon felt overwhelmed with the task at hand. My original goal seemed daunting: I wanted to write one book covering three major doctrinal areas (the Godhead, the New Birth, and Separation). Because each of these subjects was so monumental in scope, I simply could not get motivated enough to "stay the course."

Eventually, a thought occurred to me. I decided to break each of these three subjects into books of their own. Doing so would condense the subject matter into "bite-sized pieces," allowing me to feel more like the task was doable.

What you hold in your hands is the third of these three volumes, each focused on helping the reader gain the proper understanding of a particular aspect of the Apostolic message. I am incredibly grateful for the multitude of testimonies from people who have read my first two books and received revelation as a result. I pray this one is at least as much of a blessing as the others seem to have been.

My intention and purpose for writing is to provide publications almost anyone can easily understand. I believe there is a genuine need to present our message in a way that remains true to "the simplicity that is in Christ" (2 Corinthians 11:3). In fact, I believe that there is a real need in our movement to produce writings which can convince doubters and strengthen believers regardless of their spiritual or educational level.

Throughout the pages of this book, therefore, I hope to present the doctrine of separation in such a way that "the wayfaring men, though fools, shall not err therein" (Isaiah 35:8). While I desire to be thorough, I have no intention of delving into a deep theological exegesis. Rather, I want to let Scripture interpret Scripture and offer answers for the "common man."

While I wrote the first two books in this series in direct response to requests made by others, this one is different. I have never felt as much compulsion to write as I have with this topic. Having been in church since the early 1970s, I have seen many changes within the Apostolic movement. Unfortunately, a large percentage of them have been negative.

The things that were preached to me as a young man are now considered "old fashioned," "outdated," and "irrelevant" by many. I have lived long enough to see men who were once very vocal in their opposition to certain things not only tolerate them but wholeheartedly embrace them! This troubles me.

Preface

My experience has been that people have abandoned so many of the standards we once held dear because there has been very little teaching on the principles behind those standards. Too often, the explanation given behind a standard was "obey them that have the rule over you" (Hebrews 13:17). While this is a valid point, it should not be the ONLY point.

I am convinced people are much more willing to do something if they understand the reason behind it. Thankfully, the Scriptures are FILLED with reasons. I have tried to provide many of them in this book.

Let me interject that I have no intention to set precise "holiness standards" in areas where the Bible is not specific. While I will discuss important principles and (from time to time) mention my own beliefs in those areas, each individual should submit to the standards held in their local assembly. It is not my place to usurp the authority of the pastor in their lives.

This book is written in a conversational manner, as opposed to a more formal writing style. While some may prefer the latter, I am intentionally avoiding that approach. My goal is to present these truths in such a way that the reader can feel we are having a personal discussion and not just being lectured.

Before beginning the studies at hand, I should take some time to provide a glimpse into my personal testimony. I was not born into an Apostolic home. While my parents considered themselves Christians, they were not "practicing" any particular religion. They instilled in us a belief in God, but that was about as far as it went. They did not teach us about the Bible, and they did not take us to church.

Through a series of events, God brought my family to a place of desperation. We went from having a comfortable income to extreme poverty in a matter of months. When I was 11, an older cousin invited me to go with him to an Apostolic church. I agreed to go and loved it. We lived close enough that I could walk to church if necessary, and shortly after turning 12, I was baptized in Jesus' name and filled with the Holy Ghost. That summer, I felt God's call to preach. Within a few months of my conversion, my parents, siblings, and grandmother were subsequently converted. About a year after I prayed through, I preached my first sermon at the age of 13.

Not long after that, a friend took me to a debate between an Apostolic preacher and a preacher from another denomination. I watched as the Apostolic preacher quoted Scriptures and defended the message, doing it all without hesitation. Awe gripped my heart, and I was overcome with the conviction, "If he can know our doctrine that well, so can I." After attending several of these debates, I began my quest for doctrinal knowledge and understanding.

By the age of 14, I had compiled eight typed pages explaining why we baptize in Jesus' name. Three years later, during the summer between my junior and senior years in high school, I was invited to be the guest on a Christian radio talk show in Dallas, Texas, debating the subject of baptism. Within 10 years of that, God helped me convert a Trinitarian pastor, baptizing his entire family and several of his former members! Now, all these years later, the Lord has blessed me to be a part of a revival of Biblical proportions where hundreds upon hundreds are coming to the knowledge of the truth!

I only relate these things to show how Apostolic doctrine has been the focal point of my life and ministry for many years. I am certain some will find what I write to be elementary, and I am okay with that. I do not claim to be producing a doctoral thesis filled with profundities twice profounded. I am just a man with a strong passion for the truth who wants to help others comprehend it, accept it, believe it, obey it, and, most of all, love it!

There is a difference between knowledge and understanding. A person can know certain facts but not necessarily understand the meaning of those facts. For example, many high school graduates possess the knowledge that $E=mc^2$. Nevertheless, many of those same graduates do not understand what those symbols mean.

My desire is that the contents of this book will do more than simply provide you with a knowledge of the subject at hand. I hope it will also give you an in-depth understanding.

I sincerely pray God will use this book for His glory and many will receive a revelation of the truth concerning separation and holiness as a result of reading it. If even one person is convinced, convicted, or converted, my time and effort will have been worth it. May God turn many hearts back to "the old paths, where is the good way, and walk therein," and in so doing, find rest for their souls. (See Jeremiah 6:16.)

THE PREMIER PRINCIPLES

Hebrews 5:12
For when for the time ye ought to be teachers, ye have need that one teach you again which be the first principles of the oracles of God; and are become such as have need of milk, and not of strong meat.

Hebrews 6:1-2
Therefore leaving the principles of the doctrine of Christ, let us go on unto perfection; not laying again the foundation of repentance from dead works, and of faith toward God, ²Of the doctrine of baptisms, and of laying on of hands, and of resurrection of the dead, and of eternal judgment.

In Hebrews 5:12, the author mentions "the first principles of the oracles of God." The word "oracle" means a divine utterance.

In Hebrews 6:1, he mentions "the principles of the doctrine of Christ." "Principles," however, is actually the same word that was translated as "first" in Hebrews 5:12. The Greek word is "arche," which means the beginning or origin, the first in a series.[1]

"Doctrine" in this verse is translated from the Greek word

---

[1] Thayer, J., *A Greek-English Lexicon of the New Testament,* Baker Book House, 1993.

"logos" rather than "didache," which is the word that is typically used. ("Didache" means "teaching.") "Logos," as it is used here, means an utterance. Thus, both verses refer to the "first utterances" or "first principles" (as the King James Version puts it).

It seems obvious that certain principles take precedence – they are considered "first" among the others. With that being the case, we should learn to put more emphasis on – and give even greater heed to – the "first" principles. These are, by definition, the premier points providing a beginning for a series of other points which derive their origin from the "first" things. While the others are important, their importance is based upon the GREATER importance of their point of origin.

In this opening chapter, I want to address four of these "first (or premier) principles." In doing so, I hope to show you the importance God placed on them and how important they should be to us. Furthermore, establishing the significance of these particular principles will help to set the stage for the remainder of this book.

First, let us consider our Premier Doctrine. By that, I mean our primary message, which is the most essential aspect of truly Apostolic teaching.

Mark 12:29
And Jesus answered him, The first of all the commandments is, Hear, O Israel; The Lord our God is one Lord:

According to the Lord Jesus Himself, our premier doctrine is the declaration of the Oneness of God! Everything else we believe is based on this teaching.

We baptize in Jesus' name because there is only one God – if you are not baptized in that singular name, you are not baptized in the name of God! We preach the necessity of the Holy Ghost because there is only one God – if you don't have the Holy Ghost, you don't have God! Because we have a unique message of oneness, we must be unified and unique in our lifestyle.

The message of the Mighty God in Christ is a matter of salvific essentiality. Jesus stated, "If ye believe not that I am ..., ye shall die in your sins" (John 8:24). The word "he" was added by the translators. Therefore, the original statement was that you must believe Jesus is "I Am" – the same "I Am" Who spoke to Moses from the burning bush – or you will die in your sins![2]

Next, let us consider our Premier Focus. I am referring to our FIRST objective as children of God.

> **Matthew 6:33**
> *But seek ye first the kingdom of God, and his righteousness; and all these things shall be added unto you.*

Jesus clearly instructed His followers to seek God's Kingdom and righteousness. However, He did not just say we should seek this. He said we are to seek it first.

Whatever else we may pursue in this life, NOTHING should take precedence over God's Kingdom and His righteousness. Every other area of our lives ought to be governed by a driving desire to promote, propagate, and preserve the Kingdom of God! Where we work, where we live, how we spend our time, how we interact with others, and how we respond to the situations of life ought to ALL be with a single focus – a desire to benefit God's Kingdom!

Another point for our consideration is our Premier Responsibility. This should be our FIRST obligation.

> **1 Timothy 2:1**
> *I exhort therefore, that, first of all,*

---

[2] For more information on the Oneness of God and/or salvation, see my books, *Understanding the Godhead* and *Understanding the New Birth*, both available at http://www.olathetruth.com/resources

> *supplications, prayers, intercessions, and giving of thanks, be made for all men;*

Before doing anything else, we should begin every day with prayer. We cannot hope to please God if we don't stay in constant, consistent communication with Him. We cannot "walk in the Spirit" if we do not "pray in the Spirit." Regardless of what else we do FOR God, if we don't regularly spend time WITH God, our best efforts will be in vain!

In this list of four "first principles," three concern us; the fourth one involves God. Inasmuch as it says something about His nature, however, it also affects us. In fact, it probably has a GREATER effect on us than all of the other three combined!

I don't have a scripture using the word "first" to prove this is a "premier principle." Nevertheless, it is evident from the prominent place it has in Scripture that it is, indeed, a "first."

Before identifying this "premier characteristic," let us consider one of the things Jesus instructed us to include in our prayers. We find it in what we call "the Lord's Prayer."

> **Matthew 6:10**
>
> *Thy kingdom come. Thy will be done in earth, as it is in heaven.*

Based on this verse, we know that whatever happens in Heaven IS the will of God. We also see that whatever occurs in Heaven is what God WANTS on earth. With that in mind, let us look at two examples of what is happening in Heaven.

> **Isaiah 6:1-3**
>
> *In the year that king Uzziah died I saw also the Lord sitting upon a throne, high and lifted up, and his train filled the temple. ²Above it stood the seraphims: each one had six wings; with twain he covered his face, and with twain he covered his feet, and with twain he did fly. ³And one cried*

> *unto another, and said, Holy, holy, holy, is the LORD of hosts: the whole earth is full of his glory.*

> **Revelation 4:8**
> *And the four beasts had each of them six wings about him; and they were full of eyes within: and they rest not day and night, saying, Holy, holy, holy, Lord God Almighty, which was, and is, and is to come.*

Both the Old and New Testaments give witness to the fact that in Heaven, angelic creatures are proclaiming one – and only one – attribute of God. We know He has many attributes: love, truth, faithfulness, kindness, wisdom, omniscience, omnipotence, omnipresence, and more! Yet, out of all of His attributes, only ONE is proclaimed nonstop throughout eternity, and that is His holiness! Holiness, then, is His "preeminent" or "primary" or "premier" characteristic – above all else, God is holy!

This does not in any way diminish the other attributes; rather, it simply means His holiness is the "arche" – the origin of a series of other attributes which derive their beginning from it. While it is true that God is merciful and loving and not willing that ANY should perish, His love and mercy spring forth from His holiness and are, therefore, constrained by it!

In other words, God's love causes Him to want us to be saved and His mercy causes Him to reach us in our sin. Yet His holiness demands that our sin be dealt with so we can be saved! If not for His holiness, He would have saved us without going to Calvary; it was His holiness that demanded there be the shedding of blood to remit sin!

> **Hebrews 9:22**
> *And almost all things are by the law purged with blood; and without shedding of blood is no remission.*

The Premier Principles

For this reason, the Old and New Testaments repeat a constant command. Both covenants contain the same requirement: we are to be holy!

Leviticus 11:44-45

For I am the LORD your God: ye shall therefore sanctify yourselves, and ye shall be holy; for I am holy: neither shall ye defile yourselves with any manner of creeping thing that creepeth upon the earth. [45]For I am the LORD that bringeth you up out of the land of Egypt, to be your God: ye shall therefore be holy, for I am holy.

Leviticus 19:2

Speak unto all the congregation of the children of Israel, and say unto them, Ye shall be holy: for I the LORD your God am holy.

1 Peter 1:15-16

But as he which hath called you is holy, so be ye holy in all manner of conversation; [16]Because it is written, Be ye holy; for I am holy.

Ephesians 1:4

According as he hath chosen us in him before the foundation of the world, that we should be holy and without blame before him in love:

Ephesians 5:27

That he might present it to himself a glorious church, not having spot, or wrinkle, or any such thing; but that it should be holy and without blemish.

2 Peter 3:11

Seeing then that all these things shall be dissolved, what manner of persons ought ye to be in all holy conversation and godliness,

2 Corinthians 6:17-18

Wherefore come out from among them, and be ye separate, saith the Lord, and touch not the unclean thing; and I will receive you, ^{18}And will be a Father unto you, and ye shall be my sons and daughters, saith the Lord Almighty.

Titus 2:11-14

For the grace of God that bringeth salvation hath appeared to all men, ^{12}Teaching us that, denying ungodliness and worldly lusts, we should live soberly, righteously, and godly, in this present world; ^{13}Looking for that blessed hope, and the glorious appearing of the great God and our Saviour Jesus Christ; ^{14}Who gave himself for us, that he might redeem us from all iniquity, and purify unto himself a peculiar people, zealous of good works.

We MUST be holy because God is – first and foremost – a HOLY God! Even His power is associated with His holiness (and the proclamation and practice thereof).

Isaiah 6:3-4

And one cried unto another, and said, Holy, holy, holy, is the LORD of hosts: the whole earth is full of his glory. ^{4}And the posts of the door moved at the voice of him that cried, and the house was filled with smoke.

Notice how "the posts of the door moved at the voice of him that cried." Notice also what they said that brought such power. They proclaimed, "Holy, Holy, Holy!" As they did, things began to move in God's house!

Consider the man Christ Jesus. He was the seed of David

"according to the flesh," but He was the Son of God "with power, according to the spirit of holiness"!

> **Romans 1:3-4**
> *Concerning his Son Jesus Christ our Lord, which was made of the seed of David according to the flesh; ⁴And declared to be the Son of God* **with power, <u>according to the spirit of holiness</u>**, *by the resurrection from the dead:* [Emphasis added.]

As the church, we are the sons of God (see 1 John 3:1). We cannot experience God's power if we don't practice God's holiness!

He loves us enough to save us as we are, but He loves us too much to leave us as we are! He doesn't just want to save us from Hell; He wants to save us from ungodliness so we can have true fellowship and communion with Him.

When the angel announced His coming birth to Joseph, he declared that Christ would come for ONE REASON. Pay attention to what that reason is.

> **Matthew 1:21**
> *And she shall bring forth a son, and thou shalt call his name JESUS: for he shall save his people from their sins.*

Jesus didn't come to save us IN our sin or WITH our sin. Rather, He came to save us FROM our sin!

There is a principle found in the book of Amos that we should consider. Although you may be familiar with this verse, perhaps you've never considered it from this perspective.

> ***Amos 3:3***
> *Can two walk together, except they be agreed?*

Dr. Albert Barnes says the idea behind this verse is that "neither will God be with thee, unless thou art agreed and of one mind with God. Think not to have God with thee, unless thou art with God."³ In other words, if we want to walk with God, we have to be in agreement with Him. The doctrines God considers "premier" must become so to us! The "premier" characteristic in God's nature must also become ours! Until you are living in agreement with God's holiness, you will never truly "walk together" with Him!

As I bring this chapter to a close, let me summarize the four principles that should take precedence in governing both our beliefs and our behavior. To begin with, our Premier Doctrine (our PRIMARY MESSAGE) is the declaration of the Oneness of God. Our Premier Focus (our PRIMARY OBJECTIVE) is promoting, propagating, and preserving the Kingdom of God. Our Premier Responsibility (our PRIMARY OBLIGATION) is prayer and supplication. Last but certainly not least, God's Premier Attribute (His PRIMARY CHARACTERISTIC) is His holiness.

Interestingly, the Bible associates each of the first three principles with the final one. God is "the Holy One" (Job 6:10; Isaiah 40:25, 49:7; Habakkuk 1:12; 1 John 2:20). His Kingdom is associated with His righteousness (Matthew 6:33; Romans 14:17; Hebrews 1:8) and His holiness (Psalm 89:18; Isaiah 43:15). We should offer our prayers with "holy hands" (1 Timothy 2:8) and build up our "holy faith" (Jude 1:20).

This is the reason I have felt such compulsion to write this book. As more and more people (and even entire churches and church organizations) abandon holiness, there is a desperate need for the people of God to understand WHY we must be holy. It is the Premier Attribute of God Himself. Do not misunderstand – you can appear holy and not have God, but you CANNOT have God and not be holy. To abandon holiness is to abandon Him. To

---

³ Barnes, A., J. G. Murphy, F. C. Cook, E. B. Pusey, H.C. Leupold, & R. Frew, *Barnes' Notes*. Blackie & Son, 1847.

embrace Him is to embrace holiness.

May God stir up in each of us a deep desire to be holy as He is holy. One thing is certain – the Lord has promised that those who "hunger and thirst" for His righteousness "shall be filled" (Matthew 5:6)!

TRANSFORMED, NOT CONFORMED

Romans 7:15-25 (CEV)

In fact, I don't understand why I act the way I do. I don't do what I know is right. I do the things I hate. [16]Although I don't do what I know is right, I agree that the Law is good. [17]So I am not the one doing these evil things. The sin that lives in me is what does them. [18]I know that my selfish desires won't let me do anything that is good. Even when I want to do right, I cannot. [19]Instead of doing what I know is right, I do wrong. [20]And so, if I don't do what I know is right, I am no longer the one doing these evil things. The sin that lives in me is what does them. [21]The Law has shown me that something in me keeps me from doing what I know is right. [22]With my whole heart I agree with the Law of God. [23]But in every part of me I discover something fighting against my mind, and it makes me a prisoner of sin that controls everything I do. [24]What a miserable person I am. Who will rescue me from this body that is doomed to die? [25]Thank God! Jesus Christ will rescue me. So with my mind I serve the Law of God, although my selfish desires make me serve the law of sin.[4]

It is inarguable that a battle is raging between the flesh and

---

[4] *The Holy Bible: The Common English Bible,* Abingdon Press, 2011

the spirit. The Apostle Paul describes this battle in the passage above.

Notice Paul's mention of "the law of sin." We must recognize that this is more than a "problem." The pull of sin in our lives is the result of a law.

To better explain this, consider the "law" of gravity. It affects everyone, and there is no way to escape it. The way to overcome that law is by a higher law – the law of aerodynamics. Nevertheless, the law of gravity is still present. If, for example, the engine of a jet plane stops, gravity immediately takes over.

So it is with the "law" of sin in our lives. There is a constant pull on our flesh to do those things which displease God. We cannot escape the law of sin, except by the power of a higher law – the "law of the Spirit of life in Christ Jesus" (Romans 8:2)!

In chapter eight, Paul further informs us that giving in to the flesh (i.e., not overcoming the law of sin) has dire consequences. It will ultimately end in death.

Romans 8:6-7

For to be carnally minded is death; but to be spiritually minded is life and peace. ⁷Because the carnal mind is enmity against God: for it is not subject to the law of God, neither indeed can be.

With such a dreadful outcome assured, it is vital we take the proper steps to avoid it. This is the reason the Apostle Paul clearly commanded that we "be not conformed to this world."

Romans 12:2

And be not conformed to this world: but be ye transformed by the renewing of your mind, that ye may prove what is that good, and acceptable, and perfect, will of God.

The word "conformed" is a compound Greek word. The first part speaks of "association, companionship, process, or resemblance." The second means "external condition or fashion." The resulting combination would mean "a resemblance to the external fashion."

Thus, when Paul said, "Be not conformed to this world," he was saying, "Don't try to resemble the external fashions of this world!" That is why we must "present our BODIES a living sacrifice, HOLY, ACCEPTABLE UNTO GOD!" (See Romans 12:1.) We must determine that we will NOT "be conformed" to this world but will be separate and distinct instead.

> *2 Corinthians 6:17-18*
> *Wherefore come out from among them, and be ye separate, saith the Lord, and touch not the unclean thing; and I will receive you, ^{18}And will be a Father unto you, and ye shall be my sons and daughters, saith the Lord Almighty.*

However, Paul did not stop with the NEGATIVE command, telling us only what NOT to do. He went on to tell us what TO do.

> *Romans 12:2*
> *And be not conformed to this world: but be ye transformed by the renewing of your mind, that ye may prove what is that good, and acceptable, and perfect, will of God.*

We should NOT be "conformed" to the world. Rather, we SHOULD be "transformed" by the Spirit!

"Transform," in the original Greek, is the word from which we get our English word "metamorphosis." A metamorphosis is "a complete change of form, structure, or substance."[5] An example of this would be what the aquatic tadpole experiences when changing to an air-breathing frog. Another example is the

---

[5] "Metamorphosis." Dictionary.com, www.dictionary.com/browse/metamorphosis.

drastic change that allows a caterpillar to become a butterfly.

To be transformed means to undergo a spiritual metamorphosis. It requires a total and complete change.

The change in a Christian's life causes him to often be at odds with the world around him. Because of this, he may find himself in a real spiritual battle that he cannot fully understand or explain.

As the children of God, we must recognize that we face three powerful entities which are out to destroy our souls: the flesh, the devil, and the world. When any of these forces are allowed to go unchecked in our lives, we will face inevitable defeat. Only by crucifying our flesh, overcoming the devil, and separating from the world can we hope to live a spiritually victorious life.

We should note that these forces work together in an attempt to bring us down. The flesh is naturally attracted to the things of this world. The world is controlled by the power of the devil, whom Paul called "the god of this world" (2 Corinthians 4:4). Therefore, the way to keep from being influenced by the world and the devil is to crucify the carnal nature of the flesh.

James 4:7-10

Submit yourselves therefore to God. Resist the devil, and he will flee from you. ⁸Draw nigh to God, and he will draw nigh to you. Cleanse your hands, ye sinners; and purify your hearts, ye double minded. ⁹Be afflicted, and mourn, and weep: let your laughter be turned to mourning, and your joy to heaviness. ¹⁰Humble yourselves in the sight of the Lord, and he shall lift you up.

The world has no attraction to those who are dead to sin. Only when we are crucified with Christ can we hope to be free from the entanglements of sin.

Romans 6:1-2

What shall we say then? Shall we continue in

sin, that grace may abound? ²*God forbid. How shall we, that are dead to sin, live any longer therein?*

Galatians 6:14

But God forbid that I should glory, save in the cross of our Lord Jesus Christ, by whom the world is crucified unto me, and I unto the world.

Galatians 2:20

I am crucified with Christ: nevertheless I live; yet not I, but Christ liveth in me: and the life which I now live in the flesh I live by the faith of the Son of God, who loved me, and gave himself for me.

When we crucify our flesh, we are destroying the allure of this world. We begin to love what God loves and hate what God hates.

This brings us to an interesting contrast found in the Word of God. At first glance, it almost appears to be a contradiction. However, a closer examination proves that it is not the case.

In his gospel, John wrote often about God's love. In what may be the most well-known verse in his gospel (among many denominations, at least), the apostle made a notable statement regarding that love.

John 3:16

For God so loved the world, that he gave his only begotten Son, that whosoever believeth in him should not perish, but have everlasting life.

Here, John stated that God loved the world. When writing his epistle, however, he gave instructions to God's people that may seem contrary to what he said in his gospel.

> **1 John 2:15**
>
> *Love not the world, neither the things that are in the world. If any man love the world, the love of the Father is not in him.*

The way to reconcile these two verses is, first of all, by noticing that God's love toward the world was such that it caused Him to GIVE. What John warns US against involves loving the "things that are in the world." In other words, he is telling us not to love the world for what we can GET.

This is proven by looking at the verse that follows 1 John 2:15. There, John provides a definition of the "world" of which he was writing.

> **1 John 2:16**
>
> *For all that is in the world, the lust of the flesh, and the lust of the eyes, and the pride of life, is not of the Father, but is of the world.*

John 3:16 states God's love for the world involved loving the PEOPLE in the world enough to GIVE them redemption. 1 John 2:15-16 shows that the children of God should avoid the kind of love for the world that involves loving the THINGS in the world. Such love is based on the lust of the flesh, the lust of the eyes, and the pride of life. THAT is the kind of "love of the world" which is prohibited among God's people.

While dealing with 1 John 2:16, let us consider the three things John identified as worldly elements. First, he spoke of the lust of the flesh, which is simply the carnal cravings of our body to do those things which are not pleasing to God. Then, he mentioned the lust of the eyes. This can be defined as the use of our visual senses to appeal to our carnal impulses. In other words, it involves sinful temptations which come through the things we see.

The last thing John addressed in this verse requires little

explanation but may very well be the most dangerous. The pride of life can often overtake us without us even realizing it has happened. It takes on forms we sometimes fail to recognize. For instance, the refusal to admit wrongdoing is often the result of pride. The unwillingness to ask for forgiveness or try to make peace with an estranged brother or sister is usually because of pride. Stubbornness and rebellion are almost (if not entirely) always the outcropping of the pride of life.

Satan employed these three sources of evil throughout the Scripture. We find two examples in Eve's temptation in the Garden of Eden and Christ's temptation in the wilderness.

> ***Genesis 3:6***
> *And when the woman saw that the tree was good for food, and that it was pleasant to the eyes, and a tree to be desired to make one wise, she took of the fruit thereof, and did eat, and gave also unto her husband with her; and he did eat.*

In Eve's temptation, the enemy appealed to the lust of her flesh by showing her that the forbidden fruit was "good for food." The lust of the eyes was employed inasmuch as the Bible says it was "pleasant to the eyes." The pride of life came into play when Even realized the fruit was "desired to make one wise."

> ***Luke 4:3-10***
> *And the devil said unto him, If thou be the Son of God, command this stone that it be made bread. ⁴And Jesus answered him, saying, It is written, That man shall not live by bread alone, but by every word of God. ⁵And the devil, taking him up into an high mountain, shewed unto him all the kingdoms of the world in a moment of time. ⁶And the devil said unto him, All this power will I give thee, and the glory of them: for that is delivered unto me; and to whomsoever I will I*

> give it. ⁷*If thou therefore wilt worship me, all shall be thine. ⁸And Jesus answered and said unto him, Get thee behind me, Satan: for it is written, Thou shalt worship the Lord thy God, and him only shalt thou serve. ⁹And he brought him to Jerusalem, and set him on a pinnacle of the temple, and said unto him, If thou be the Son of God, cast thyself down from hence: ¹⁰For it is written, He shall give his angels charge over thee, to keep thee:*

We see the same three forces at work during the temptation of Christ. When the devil tried to get the Lord to turn the stones into bread at the end of a fast, he was using the lust of the flesh. He then offered the kingdoms of this world by taking Christ to a high place and showing him these kingdoms, thus making an appeal through the lust of the eyes. In his final attempt, the devil told the Lord to cast Himself down so that angels could come and bear Him up. This would no doubt have brought much attention to the man Christ Jesus, meaning Satan was trying to employ the pride of life.

Just as he did with Eve and Jesus, so the devil uses these same tactics to make the world more appealing to Christians. From the creation of man, to the coming of the Savior, and to this present time, the methods the enemy uses have not changed. This is why Paul said, "We are not ignorant of [the devil's] devices" (2 Corinthians 2:11). It is incumbent upon us to resist the enemy and reject what the world and flesh throw at us.

The church must always maintain a clear line of distinction between itself and the world. There can never be fellowship between light and darkness! The two simply are not compatible.

> **2 Corinthians 6:14**
> *Be ye not unequally yoked together with unbelievers: for what fellowship hath*

> *righteousness with unrighteousness? and what communion hath light with darkness?*

If you turn on a light, the darkness HAS to disappear. That is the function of the church: to be a light dispelling the darkness of the world!

> **2 Corinthians 6:17-18**
> *Wherefore come out from among them, and be ye separate, saith the Lord, and touch not the unclean thing; and I will receive you, ^{18}And will be a Father unto you, and ye shall be my sons and daughters, saith the Lord Almighty.*

Today's church needs a fresh revelation that the promise of becoming sons and daughters of God is entirely conditional upon complete separation from the world. If God's people ever plan to be taken out of this world, we must first allow God to take the world out of us!

Separation from the world brings victory, power, and the joy of the Lord. The Christian who maintains complete separation from the world has a genuine testimony which will affect all who know him.

There is no question that separation from the world carries with it a specially designated power from the Lord. Paul stated this fact when he wrote to Timothy about those who "deny the power" of godliness (see 2 Timothy 3:5).

It is impossible to please God while trying to hang on to the things of this world. In fact, it is, quite frankly, dishonest to claim to be living "for God" while at the same time living to please our own carnal flesh. We must decide whether we will serve ourselves or serve our Creator.

> **2 Timothy 2:4**
> *No man that warreth entangleth himself with the affairs of this life; that he may please him who*

hath chosen him to be a soldier.

A person who straddles the fence between God and the world will not survive spiritually. God is trying to lead us to Heaven. The world, the devil, and our flesh are all trying to drag us to Hell. It is simply not possible to go both directions at the same time.

Matthew 6:24
No man can serve two masters: for either he will hate the one, and love the other; or else he will hold to the one, and despise the other. Ye cannot serve God and mammon.

Galatians 4:3
Even so we, when we were children, were in bondage under the elements of the world:

Galatians 4:9
But now, after that ye have known God, or rather are known of God, how turn ye again to the weak and beggarly elements, whereunto ye desire again to be in bondage?

The story is told of a cowboy in years gone by who had been an alcoholic but was eventually saved from that lifestyle. However, he continued to battle cravings for liquor and was struggling to remain sober. As it turned out, part of his problem was stopping his horse in front of the saloon and tying it to the hitching post there every time he rode into town. Growing weary and frustrated that he couldn't seem to alleviate the temptation, he finally consulted his pastor. It didn't take long for the preacher to respond, saying simply, "Get a new hitching post." Once the cowboy took the advice and began tying his horse at the other end of the street, he immediately realized he was no longer feeling the tug of the saloon every time he dismounted. The moral of this story should be clear: we cannot expect God to deliver us when we refuse to make necessary changes ourselves. Paul said we should "make not provision for the flesh, to fulfill the lusts thereof" (Romans 13:14). Only a complete separation from the world can assure us of victory.

Living close to the world is very dangerous. When a Christian lives in close proximity to the world, its attractions may easily overcome him. He may find himself dragged down into the quicksand of evil desires. The lust of the flesh and the lust of the eyes can become too strong for a weak believer, and he can be swept back into a life of sin. Just as one cannot play with fire without getting burned, so a person cannot flirt with the things that cater to the lust of the flesh without being overtaken by sin.

The physical law of gravity states that two objects attract each other inversely, proportional to the square of the distance between their centers. In other words, the closer two objects are, the stronger the attraction.

This is also true spiritually: The closer a person lives to the world, the more attracted he is to it, and the stronger he finds the pull of the world. Our obligation is to get into a spiritual orbit beyond the pull of the world.

Many years ago, I read about a man who had advertised for someone to serve as a driver for his wife and family. Many applicants desired the job, and they were all tested in the same manner.

The road narrowed along the top of a steep cliff not far from where the man lived. Each driver was instructed to drive as close to the edge of the cliff as possible without going over the edge. Each applicant took on the challenge daringly, driving ever closer to the edge of the cliff. Finally, one young man climbed into the driver's seat and went on the opposite side of the road, as far from the cliff as possible.

The young man was given the job. You see, the employer was going to trust the lives of his wife and children into the hands of whomever he hired. Accordingly, he was not interested in how close the applicant could drive to danger but instead how far he could stay away from it.

This is how we, as Christians, should live. True safety comes in putting as much distance as possible between us and temptation. The greater the distance we are FROM the world, the less attraction there is TO the world.

In the opening paragraphs of this chapter, we examined Paul's command that we "be not conformed" but rather be "transformed." We further discussed how the word "transformed" in this verse means undergoing a total and complete change of nature. Let us consider the verse in question once again.

Romans 12:2
And be not conformed to this world: but be ye transformed by the renewing of your mind, that ye may prove what is that good, and acceptable, and perfect, will of God.

The English word "transformed" is found in only one other Bible passage, which is 2 Corinthians 11. In verses 14-15, we see the word "transformed," and in verse 13, we find "transforming."

2 Corinthians 11:13-15
For such are false apostles, deceitful workers, transforming themselves into the apostles of Christ. [14]And no marvel; for Satan himself is transformed into an angel of light. [15]Therefore it is no great thing if his ministers also be transformed as the ministers of righteousness; whose end shall be according to their works.

It is noteworthy, however, that the Greek word translated "transformed" in Romans 12:2 and the Greek word translated "transformed" in 2 Corinthians 11:14-15 (and "transforming" in verse 13) are NOT the same word. These two passages use very different words with very different meanings.

Understanding Separation

While Romans 12:2 uses the Greek word *metamorphoō*, 2 Corinthians 11:13-15 uses the Greek word *metaschēmatizō*. Although both words involve a kind of change (and both words are translated as "change" in other verses), the TYPE of change indicated by the words in these verses is actually very different.

As I have already pointed out, *metamorphoō* is the word from which we get "metamorphosis" – a complete transformation in the form, structure, and substance of an organism or life form, such as when a tadpole becomes a frog or a caterpillar becomes a butterfly. M*etaschēmatizō*, on the other hand (as used in the passage in 2 Corinthians), means "to disguise." In other words, while it outwardly APPEARS there has been a change, it is ONLY outwardly – it is nothing more than a change in appearance, but NOT in nature!

In 2 Corinthians 11:13-15, the subject at hand is false teachers who "transform themselves" into something they are not. The whole purpose of this "transformation" is to deceive others. Significantly, this transformation is something they do to themselves.

In Romans 12, on the other hand, the command is that we "be transformed" – not that we transform ourselves. True transformation is not something we accomplish on our own. Far too many Apostolics try to "transform themselves" by simply adhering to a standard or obeying a mandate. Don't get me wrong; these things are necessary. However, it must go beyond simple adherence or obedience.

You can glue legs on a tadpole and cut its tail off – but that will not make it a frog. It will still be aquatic; it will still breathe through its gills and need the water to live. You can also glue wings on a caterpillar, but that will not give it the ability to fly. It may LOOK like a butterfly, but it has not undergone metamorphosis. So it is with saints who simply try to look the part.

According to Scripture, obedience is better than sacrifice (see

1 Samuel 15:22). Nevertheless, obedience alone will not work over the long term. At some point, every child of God must experience a genuine transformation, which only the power of the Spirit can accomplish!

The OTHER kind of transformation requires more than a change in appearance. It requires more than simply conforming.

> **Romans 12:2**
> *And be not conformed to this world: but be ye transformed by the renewing of your mind, that ye may prove what is that good, and acceptable, and perfect, will of God.*

Genuine transformation begins with a renewing of your mind. The word "renewing" literally means a "renovation." Your mind has to be completely overhauled to the point it can think in such a way that you seek to please God. *The New International Reader's Version* says, "Let your way of thinking be completely changed."[6]

Earlier in the Book of Romans, Paul had issued a grave warning. He informed his readers that NOT allowing our minds to be renewed would ultimately result in spiritual death.

> **Romans 8:6-7**
> *For to be carnally minded is death; but to be spiritually minded is life and peace. [7]Because the carnal mind is enmity against God: for it is not subject to the law of God, neither indeed can be.*

To fully understand verses 6 and 7, we must read the context in which they were written. Doing so will also help us grasp the significance of striving for a spiritual mind.

> **Romans 8:1-9**
> *There is therefore now no condemnation to*

---

[6] *The Holy Bible: New International Reader's Version*, Zondervan, 2016.

them which are in Christ Jesus, who walk not after the flesh, but after the Spirit. ²For the law of the Spirit of life in Christ Jesus hath made me free from the law of sin and death. ³For what the law could not do, in that it was weak through the flesh, God sending his own Son in the likeness of sinful flesh, and for sin, condemned sin in the flesh: ⁴That the righteousness of the law might be fulfilled in us, who walk not after the flesh, but after the Spirit. ⁵For they that are after the flesh do mind the things of the flesh; but they that are after the Spirit the things of the Spirit. ⁶For to be carnally minded is death; but to be spiritually minded is life and peace. ⁷Because the carnal mind is enmity against God: for it is not subject to the law of God, neither indeed can be. ⁸So then they that are in the flesh cannot please God. ⁹But ye are not in the flesh, but in the Spirit, if so be that the Spirit of God dwell in you. Now if any man have not the Spirit of Christ, he is none of his.

The way we "transform" our mind from a carnal mind to a Spiritual mind requires that we learn to quit walking according to our carnal flesh and start walking according to the will of the Spirit. As we learn to do this, our minds are being transformed from the carnal mind to the mind of Christ. All of this is predicated upon being – and remaining – full of the Spirit!

BE YE SEPARATE

2 Corinthians 6:14-18

Be ye not unequally yoked together with unbelievers: for what fellowship hath righteousness with unrighteousness? and what communion hath light with darkness? ^{15}And what concord hath Christ with Belial? or what part hath he that believeth with an infidel? ^{16}And what agreement hath the temple of God with idols? for ye are the temple of the living God; as God hath said, I will dwell in them, and walk in them; and I will be their God, and they shall be my people. ^{17}Wherefore come out from among them, and be ye separate, saith the Lord, and touch not the unclean thing; and I will receive you, ^{18}And will be a Father unto you, and ye shall be my sons and daughters, saith the Lord Almighty.

The scriptures are clear that from the very beginning, God has intended for His people to be different from anyone else. Noah found grace *because* he was different from everyone else.

Genesis 6:5-9

And God saw that the wickedness of man was great in the earth, and that every imagination of the thoughts of his heart was only evil continually. ^{6}And it repented the Lord that he had made man on the earth, and it grieved him at his heart. ^{7}And the Lord said, I will destroy man

> *whom I have created from the face of the earth; both man, and beast, and the creeping thing, and the fowls of the air; for it repenteth me that I have made them. ⁸But Noah found grace in the eyes of the Lord. ⁹These are the generations of Noah: Noah was a just man and perfect in his generations, and Noah walked with God.*

God chose Noah and extended him grace because he "walked with God." In fact, Peter referred to Noah as "a preacher of righteousness" (2 Peter 2:5). Noah lived a separated life from the rest of the world, and God blessed Him accordingly.

When God dealt with Abraham, His first commandment was for Abraham to separate himself from everyone else. In this case, it even included his own family.

> **Genesis 12:1-3**
>
> *Now the LORD had said unto Abram, Get thee out of thy country, and from thy kindred, and from thy father's house, unto a land that I will shew thee: ²And I will make of thee a great nation, and I will bless thee, and make thy name great; and thou shalt be a blessing: ³And I will bless them that bless thee, and curse him that curseth thee: and in thee shall all families of the earth be blessed.*

God repeatedly commanded Israel to be different. Just a few scriptural examples ought to suffice.

> **Leviticus 20:7**
>
> *Sanctify yourselves therefore, and be ye holy: for I am the LORD your God.*

> **Deuteronomy 26:18-19**
>
> *And the Lord hath avouched thee this day to be his peculiar people, as he hath promised thee,*

and that thou shouldest keep all his commandments; ¹⁹And to make thee high above all nations which he hath made, in praise, and in name, and in honour; and that thou mayest be an holy people unto the Lord thy God, as he hath spoken.

This was not just necessary during the Old Testament time period. The New Testament church was undeniably under the same command for separation.

1 Peter 1:15-16
But as he which hath called you is holy, so be ye holy in all manner of conversation; ¹⁶Because it is written, Be ye holy; for I am holy.

2 Corinthians 6:17-18
Wherefore come out from among them, and be ye separate, saith the Lord, and touch not the unclean thing; and I will receive you, ¹⁸And will be a Father unto you, and ye shall be my sons and daughters, saith the Lord Almighty.

Hebrews 12:14
Follow peace with all men, and holiness, without which no man shall see the Lord:

Titus 2:11-13
For the grace of God that bringeth salvation hath appeared to all men, ¹²Teaching us that, denying ungodliness and worldly lusts, we should live soberly, righteously, and godly, in this present world; ¹³Looking for that blessed hope, and the glorious appearing of the great God and our Saviour Jesus Christ;

Separation is not JUST a mindset. While some would say God only expects us to "think" differently than the world,

Scripture teaches otherwise. Our outward actions, lifestyle, and even appearance are a major part of the kind of separation God requires.

Before getting into that, however, let me stress the fact that outward appearance ALONE is NOT sufficient! We must also make sure our inner man is sanctified unto God.

> ### Matthew 23:25-27
> *Woe unto you, scribes and Pharisees, hypocrites! for ye make clean the outside of the cup and of the platter, but within they are full of extortion and excess. [26]Thou blind Pharisee, cleanse first that which is within the cup and platter, that the outside of them may be clean also. [27]Woe unto you, scribes and Pharisees, hypocrites! for ye are like unto whited sepulchres, which indeed appear beautiful outward, but are within full of dead men's bones, and of all uncleanness.*

Jesus did not say to clean only the inside and not worry about the outside. Rather, He said the PURPOSE for cleansing the inside was SO THAT the outside would also be clean. We must recognize that inward cleansing is not complete without an outward change as well. Both are essential!

> ### 1 Corinthians 6:19-20
> *What? know ye not that your body is the temple of the Holy Ghost which is in you, which ye have of God, and ye are not your own? [20]For ye are bought with a price: therefore glorify God in your body, and in your spirit, which are God's.*

The clear command is to glorify God "in your spirit" (the inside) AND "in your body" (the outside). In fact, cleansing both is described by Paul as PERFECT holiness! He stressed this in his second letter to Corinth.

> **2 Corinthians 7:1**
> *Having therefore these promises, dearly beloved, let us cleanse ourselves from all filthiness of the flesh and spirit, perfecting holiness in the fear of God.*

I contend that a significant aspect of true Apostolic preaching and teaching will consist of MUCH more time dealing with inward matters than outward appearance. However, we cannot neglect the outward appearance, as will be proven throughout the remainder of this book.

Despite what many Christian groups say today, outward appearance DOES matter to God. While they often refer to God's words to the prophet Samuel as proof of their "liberty" to dress as they please, a close examination of the verse in question plainly shows otherwise.

> **1 Samuel 16:7**
> *But the LORD said unto Samuel, Look not on his countenance, or on the height of his stature; because I have refused him: for the LORD seeth not as man seeth; for man looketh on the outward appearance, but the LORD looketh on the heart.*

In interpreting any passage of Scripture, one must always consider the context. The context of this verse shows that this is a reference to choosing a king and has nothing to do with outward holiness. Note how God speaks of man's "countenance" and "height of stature." Not once does God even deal with clothing!

At this point in history, Israel had only known one king – King Saul, of whom it was said, "from his shoulders and upward he was higher than any of the people" (1 Samuel 9:2). Thus, as Samuel was trying to figure out who would become Saul's replacement, he no doubt was using Saul's appearance as at least part of his guide. The Lord simply told him, "The next man does NOT have to 'look the part' – I'm interested in something more this time around."

To use this verse as proof that God has no interest in how we adorn ourselves is simply a misappropriation of Scripture. God was undoubtedly concerned about outward adorning, as is seen in the following examples.

- **Adam and Eve**

    Genesis 3:21
    Unto Adam also and to his wife did the LORD God make coats of skins, and clothed them.

According to Genesis 3:7, Adam and Eve had already clothed themselves. In God's eyes, however, their clothing was obviously not sufficient.

Although some people claim that the clothing was not sufficient because there needed to be the shedding of blood, this is a mere assumption that may or may not be relevant. Please pay attention to the wording of these two verses: in verse 7, they "made themselves aprons;" in verse 21, God made "coats."

Genesis 3:7
And the eyes of them both were opened, and they knew that they were naked; and they sewed fig leaves together, and made themselves aprons.

The word "apron" means a "girdle" that simply "covered the loins," while "coats" is translated from a word meaning "tunics."[7] A "tunic" is defined as "a simple slip-on garment [that is] usually knee-length or longer."[8]

It seems to me that there was much more to God's decision to replace the fig-leaf aprons with animal-skin tunics – the way

---

[7] Brown, Francis, S. R. Driver, and Charles Augustus Briggs. *A Hebrew and English Lexicon of the Old Testament*. Houghton Mifflin Company, 1906.

[8] Merriam-Webster Dictionary, https://www.merriam-webster.com/dictionary/tunic

they chose to cover themselves was not adequately modest! Remember that, at that time, there was no one in the garden except Adam, Eve, and God. The Lord was not providing additional covering so that the husband and wife would be more modest in each other's presence. Instead, He was setting an important precedent for what He expects regarding how we dress!

- **Joshua the High Priest**

    Zechariah 3:3-5

    Now Joshua was clothed with filthy garments, and stood before the angel. 4And he answered and spake unto those that stood before him, saying, Take away the filthy garments from him. And unto him he said, Behold, I have caused thine iniquity to pass from thee, and I will clothe thee with change of raiment. 5And I said, Let them set a fair mitre upon his head. So they set a fair mitre upon his head, and clothed him with garments. And the angel of the LORD stood by.

God would not allow Joshua to serve Him dressed as he was. He could only do so if his outward appearance met God's standards!

- **The Demoniac of Gadara**

    Mark 5:15

    And they come to Jesus, and see him that was possessed with the devil, and had the legion, sitting, and clothed, and in his right mind: and they were afraid.

I find it interesting that demon possession led to total nakedness. Could it be that the more a person is influenced by the devil, the more of their bodies they want to expose? Not only is this possible, I would dare say it is probable!

After an encounter with Christ, however, he was not only

delivered from demonic possession. He was not only given back his "right mind." Significantly, he was also "clothed"! Jesus obviously was looking at MORE than what was in this man's heart.

- **The Levitical Priests**

   Exodus 28:2

   And thou shalt make holy garments for Aaron thy brother for glory and for beauty.

The Lord instructed Moses that the priests were to dress for glory *first*. Beauty was a secondary matter. I believe this is a principle for which we should ALL strive! Tight-fitting, sheer, and otherwise immodest clothing certainly doesn't glorify God. These issues will be dealt with in greater detail in a later chapter.

Consider this: If outward separation is not important to God, why did He inspire the apostles to address the adornment of Christians in various passages? We will list only two, but we could just as easily add many more.

1 Timothy 2:8-10

I will therefore that men pray every where, lifting up holy hands, without wrath and doubting. ⁹In like manner also, that women adorn themselves in modest apparel, with shamefacedness and sobriety; not with broided hair, or gold, or pearls, or costly array; ¹⁰But (which becometh women professing godliness) with good works.

1 Peter 3:3-5

Whose adorning let it not be that outward adorning of plaiting the hair, and of wearing of gold, or of putting on of apparel; ⁴But let it be the hidden man of the heart, in that which is not corruptible, even the ornament of a meek and quiet spirit, which is in the sight of God of great price. ⁵For after this manner in the old time the holy women also, who trusted in God, adorned themselves, being in subjection unto their own husbands:

If outward appearance were unimportant, there would be no reason for both Paul and Peter to address the subject. Nevertheless, they did! Furthermore, Peter stressed that we should follow the examples of those who lived "in the old time." Even in current times, most devout followers of Judaism strongly resemble the very manner of dress upheld among Apostolics today!

As discussed in our very first chapter, God's premier characteristic is His holiness. It is because of His holiness that we are commanded to also be holy.

Leviticus 20:7
Sanctify yourselves therefore, and be ye holy: for I am the LORD your God.

Notice the direct correlation between "sanctifying yourselves" and "being holy." This is because the word "sanctify" means "set apart," and the word "holy" means "separate." It is impossible to "sanctify yourselves" unless you are separate from the rest of the world.

Once again, this is not just an Old Testament mandate. Rather, it is repeated in the New Testament and is, therefore, binding upon the church today.

1 Peter 1:15-16
But as he which hath called you is holy, so be ye holy in all manner of conversation; ¹⁶Because it is written, Be ye holy; for I am holy.

The apostle mandated that we must be holy "in ALL manner of conversation." The word "conversation" means "manner of life, behavior, conduct."[9] Thus, separation does NOT just involve our attitude and outlook (although those are important), but in ALL MANNERS OF LIFESTYLE – including our outward appearance!

---

[9] Thayer, J., *A Greek-English Lexicon of the New Testament,* Baker Book House, 1993.

A RIGHT SPIRIT

Psalms 51:7-13
Purge me with hyssop, and I shall be clean: wash me, and I shall be whiter than snow. [8]Make me to hear joy and gladness; that the bones which thou hast broken may rejoice. [9]Hide thy face from my sins, and blot out all mine iniquities. [10]Create in me a clean heart, O God; and renew a right spirit within me. [11]Cast me not away from thy presence; and take not thy holy spirit from me. [12]Restore unto me the joy of thy salvation; and uphold me with thy free spirit. [13]Then will I teach transgressors thy ways; and sinners shall be converted unto thee.

In this prayer of repentance, King David specifically asked God to do two things. First, he wanted God to create a clean heart in him. Pay attention to the fact that he didn't ask God to cleanse his heart. He asked for God to create a clean one. David obviously recognized something was wrong with the heart he had inasmuch as he had done such wicked things as adultery and intentional manslaughter. Just cleaning his heart was not sufficient.

The second request was that God "renew" a right spirit in him. He understood that his spirit needed correction. While the word often signifies to rebuild or restore, in this particular passage, it actually carries the connotation of "producing something new."[10]

From the Psalmist's perspective, just being forgiven of a transgression was not enough. He wanted God to ensure his spirit and heart were right so he would not repeat his offenses.

In our last chapter, we briefly mentioned the concept of "perfect holiness." Let us look at this idea a little more closely.

> ***2 Corinthians 7:1***
> *Having therefore these promises, dearly beloved, let us cleanse ourselves from all filthiness of the flesh and spirit, perfecting holiness in the fear of God.*

In this verse, the word "perfect" does NOT speak of flawlessness but rather "completion." Therefore, "perfect holiness" simply means "complete holiness." According to Paul, perfect holiness requires being cleansed from the filthiness of both flesh AND spirit!

> ***1 Thessalonians 5:23***
> *And the very God of peace sanctify you wholly; and I pray God your whole spirit and soul and body be preserved blameless unto the coming of our Lord Jesus Christ.*

Notice how Paul spoke of both the body AND the spirit being preserved blameless. While I will spend a great deal of time in this book addressing the importance of outward holiness, please let me be clear: outward holiness is absolutely wasted if it is not accompanied by inward holiness!

> ***Matthew 23:23-28***
> *Woe unto you, scribes and Pharisees, hypocrites! for ye pay tithe of mint and anise and*

---

[10] Barnes, A., J. G. Murphy, F. C. Cook, E. B. Pusey, H.C. Leupold, & R. Frew, *Barnes' Notes*. Blackie & Son, 1847.

> cummin, and have omitted the weightier matters of the law, judgment, mercy, and faith: these ought ye to have done, and not to leave the other undone. ^{24}Ye blind guides, which strain at a gnat, and swallow a camel. ^{25}Woe unto you, scribes and Pharisees, hypocrites! for ye make clean the outside of the cup and of the platter, but within they are full of extortion and excess. ^{26}Thou blind Pharisee, cleanse first that which is within the cup and platter, that the outside of them may be clean also. ^{27}Woe unto you, scribes and Pharisees, hypocrites! for ye are like unto whited sepulchres, which indeed appear beautiful outward, but are within full of dead men's bones, and of all uncleanness. ^{28}Even so ye also outwardly appear righteous unto men, but within ye are full of hypocrisy and iniquity.

Jesus condemned the Pharisees, not for their outward holiness but for their inward filthiness. He instructed them that they were NOT to quit doing the outward things, but they should FIRST correct things inwardly. We, too, must be very careful in our quest for separation so that we do not neglect the pursuit of inward holiness while focusing solely on outward holiness!

What good does it do for an Apostolic lady to have long hair, long sleeves, long skirts, and also have a long tongue? Our outer appearance means nothing if our inner man is corrupt! Just because we look the part does not mean God is pleased.

Furthermore, just because something is done in the right way doesn't mean it's done with a right spirit! The following passage from the Book of Acts proves this point.

Acts 16:16-18
> And it came to pass, as we went to prayer, a certain damsel possessed with a spirit of

> divination met us, which brought her masters much gain by soothsaying: ¹⁷The same followed Paul and us, and cried, saying, These men are the servants of the most high God, which shew unto us the way of salvation. ¹⁸And this did she many days. But Paul, being grieved, turned and said to the spirit, I command thee in the name of Jesus Christ to come out of her. And he came out the same hour.

Identifying these apostles as "servants of the most high God" who would show "the way of salvation" was the right thing. The spirit driving her, however, was NOT right! Thus, it is very possible for us to do the right thing (such as dressing right, coming to church, or paying our tithes) but to do so with a wrong spirit.

Make no mistake: maintaining a right spirit is absolutely essential. God fully expects us to do those things He commands, but we must do them with the right spirit.

Proverbs 25:28
> He that hath no rule over his own spirit is like a city that is broken down, and without walls.

In ancient times, the first line of defense in the protection of a city consisted of the walls built around that city. The Book of Proverbs says the lack of control over our spirit is the same as a city with no way to defend itself against the enemy's attacks. Keeping a right spirit provides protection against the spiritual forces which oppose us.

There is a simple reason why this is true. Our spirit affects everything in our life. The following story illustrates this fact.

"Because of the unhappiness within us, we see everything in a negative vein. I am told that a drunk one time passed out on a sidewalk. A prankster decided to rub Limburger cheese into his thick mustache. When he aroused from his stupor, a few breaths caused him to wrinkle his nose in disgust and say, 'Boy, it stinks here. It smells like Limburger cheese. I'm going out to the park where it won't smell so much. To his surprise, when he got to the park, he still smelled Limburger cheese. He decided to go further out into the country, but there he found the scent unchanged. 'It's terrible!' he exclaimed. 'The whole world smells like Limburger cheese!' His perception was that everything was bad, but the trouble was right under his nose. Likewise, those who allow their spirit to become damaged perceive that there is something wrong with everybody and everything when the trouble is right under their nose."[11]

It has been said that cursing the darkness is useless unless you're willing to offer some light. Therefore, I don't want to simply tell you to refrain from having a bad spirit. Instead, I want to take some time to share a couple of specific things you can do to help you keep your spirit right.

- **Focus on God.**

    Isaiah 26:3

    Thou wilt keep him in perfect peace, whose mind is stayed on thee: because he trusteth in thee.

    No matter what is happening in our lives, God is always good. When life's not good, God still is! "He is loving, perfect, and altogether righteous. He never leaves us or forsakes us (see Hebrews 13:5). When we find ourselves becoming negative or discouraged, we haven't focused enough attention on God." [12]

- **Keep the right friends.**

    Proverbs 27:17

    Iron sharpeneth iron; so a man sharpeneth the

---

[11] Oullette, Dr. R. B., Ministry 127, https://ministry127.com/christian-living/keeping-your-spirit-right

[12] *Ibid.*

countenance of his friend.

Proverbs 27:9
Ointment and perfume rejoice the heart: so doth the sweetness of a man's friend by hearty counsel.

As one writer put it, "Having friends with good spirits, right attitudes, and good hearts will do much to keep us on the right path and in the right attitude. Spend time with people who lift your spirits, not those who tear you down."[13]

As I continue to reiterate, our outward appearance DOES matter. Still, if our INWARD man is not right, our outward appearance matters little. The Apostle Peter makes it clear that "the hidden man of the heart" is far more important than our "outward adorning."

1 Peter 3:3-4
Whose adorning let it not be that outward adorning of plaiting the hair, and of wearing of gold, or of putting on of apparel; ⁴But let it be the hidden man of the heart, in that which is not corruptible, even the ornament of a meek and quiet spirit, which is in the sight of God of great price.

The fact is, we are to be clothed with HIS holiness. The Prophet Isaiah addressed this principle.

Isaiah 61:10
I will greatly rejoice in the LORD, my soul shall be joyful in my God; for he hath clothed me with the garments of salvation, he hath covered me with the robe of righteousness, as a

---

[13] Oullette, Dr. R. B., Ministry 127, https://ministry127.com/christian-living/keeping-your-spirit-right

> *bridegroom decketh himself with ornaments, and as a bride adorneth herself with her jewels.*

If we are not clothed with HIS holiness, any attempts at separation are nothing more than self-righteousness. God not only disapproves of this – He sees it as loathsome.

> ***Isaiah 64:6***
> *But we are all as an unclean thing, and all our righteousnesses are as filthy rags; and we all do fade as a leaf; and our iniquities, like the wind, have taken us away.*

The key to understanding this verse is the possessive pronoun "our." It is "our" righteousnesses that seem to God as "filthy rags." The concept behind the term "filthy rags" is literally something which was to be considered abominable or detestable to the Levitical priesthood. God sees our human attempts at righteousness in the same way. It is disgusting to Him. What we need is HIS holiness, which He must impart to us by giving us a clean heart and a right spirit!

The fact is, if outward separation alone made us holy, then groups like the Amish and Mennonites would be more holy than any of us. Again, this is NOT intended to discount the importance of separation – if it were, this book would not be written! Instead, I am simply stressing that whatever separation we exhibit should be the result of a spirit of holiness.

A typical attack many people make against those of us who promote and/or adhere to principles of separation is they refer to us as "Pharisees." In the minds of many, it seems nothing could be worse than being a "Pharisaical Christian." In fact, the word "Pharisaical" is defined as "marked by hypocritical censorious self-righteousness."[14]

---

[14] Merriam-Webster Dictionary, https://www.merriam-webster.com

A Right Spirit

This is based mainly on a perception that Christ's criticism of the Pharisees of the New Testament came because they practiced outward holiness. While there is no question that Jesus warned against certain aspects associated with the Pharisees, His condemnation was not because they were living separated lives.

The attacks made today ignore (or overlook) two critical facts. First, Jesus commanded His disciples to obey the Pharisees.

Matthew 23:2-3
Saying, The scribes and the Pharisees sit in Moses' seat: ³All therefore whatsoever they bid you observe, that observe and do; but do not ye after their works: for they say, and do not.

Although He DID condemn some of their actions, He did NOT condemn their rules and guidelines. He actually taught that they were to be followed. He condemned the fact that they preached things they did not practice. It was their open hypocrisy He deplored, NOT their outward holiness!

The second thing people seem to fail to take into account is that the great Apostle Paul was NOT ashamed to be a Pharisee. Instead, he seemed to wear it as a badge of honor.

Philippians 3:5
Circumcised the eighth day, of the stock of Israel, of the tribe of Benjamin, an Hebrew of the Hebrews; as touching the law, a Pharisee;

The problem with the Pharisees was not that they were living a life of separation. It was that they were so focused on the "letter of the law" that they neglected the "spirit of the law."

2 Corinthians 3:6
Who also hath made us able ministers of the new testament; not of the letter, but of the spirit: for the letter killeth, but the spirit giveth life.

Holiness must start from within. As one preacher said,

"Without the proper mindset and attitudes, we can never be holy, even if we conform to a form of outward holiness."[15]

He went on to say, "Holy living does not consist of conforming to standards to make a show of holiness, to be seen by others, or to seem spiritual. Rather, true holiness stems from a deep, heartfelt desire to live in such a way that is pleasing to God every day."[16]

True holiness will be reflected in our outward appearance. It will be a result of a deep, inward desire.

When addressing the Pharisees, Jesus plainly taught that simply living up to a standard outwardly does NOT equate with truly being holy. It involves far more.

> **Matthew 5:21-22**
>
> *Ye have heard that it was said by them of old time, Thou shalt not kill; and whosoever shall kill shall be in danger of the judgment: ^{22}But I say unto you, That whosoever is angry with his brother without a cause shall be in danger of the judgment: and whosoever shall say to his brother, Raca, shall be in danger of the council: but whosoever shall say, Thou fool, shall be in danger of hell fire.*
>
> **Matthew 5:27-28**
>
> *Ye have heard that it was said by them of old time, Thou shalt not commit adultery: ^{28}But I say unto you, That whosoever looketh on a woman to lust after her hath committed adultery with her already in his heart.*

---

[15] Stewart, Missionary Jessie, *Inward Holiness,* taught at a conference in the Republic of South Africa on March 28, 2024.

[16] *Ibid.*

A Right Spirit

Although the Pharisees believed themselves to be holy because they refused to kill someone, Jesus said you're doing the same thing in your spirit when you hate them. Just because they didn't commit the physical act of adultery did not mean they hadn't been guilty of that sin in a spiritual sense.

We must never reach a place where we focus SOLELY on our outward appearance. If we do, we will be judged in the same way Jesus judged the Pharisees.

Matthew 23:27-28
Woe unto you, scribes and Pharisees, hypocrites! for ye are like unto whited sepulchres, which indeed appear beautiful outward, but are within full of dead men's bones, and of all uncleanness. [28]Even so ye also outwardly appear righteous unto men, but within ye are full of hypocrisy and iniquity.

Unfortunately, too many Apostolics are so consumed with examining someone's outward appearance that they neglect the importance of inward holiness. We can easily think someone is spiritual based on our limited perspective, but God does not share this limitation. Instead, He is able to look inwardly and see what is in a man's heart.

1 Samuel 16:7
But the LORD said unto Samuel, Look not on his countenance, or on the height of his stature; because I have refused him: for the LORD seeth not as man seeth; for man looketh on the outward appearance, but the LORD looketh on the heart.

Again, this does NOT mean God DOESN'T see the outward appearance. It simply means the outward appearance ALONE is not sufficient to please Him!

The underlying problem with humanity is our very nature is

carnal. From the moment of conception, there is within us the propensity and desire for – and, therefore, the inclination toward – sinful things and ungodly lifestyles.

Psalms 51:5
Behold, I was shapen in iniquity; and in sin did my mother conceive me.

Sin is in our nature. As a result, we naturally produce "the works of the flesh."

Galatians 5:19-21
Now the works of the flesh are manifest, which are these; Adultery, fornication, uncleanness, lasciviousness, [20]Idolatry, witchcraft, hatred, variance, emulations, wrath, strife, seditions, heresies, [21]Envyings, murders, drunkenness, revellings, and such like: of the which I tell you before, as I have also told you in time past, that they which do such things shall not inherit the kingdom of God.

Some of the things listed involve outward sins, but not all of them. Many deal with the spirit and the inner man.

As I previously stated, the Bible teaches we must be "transformed." We must be completely changed!

Romans 12:2
And be not conformed to this world: but be ye transformed by the renewing of your mind, that ye may prove what is that good, and acceptable, and perfect, will of God.

Such a transformation is only possible through the power of the Spirit. It will result in putting sinful deeds to death.

Romans 8:13
For if ye live after the flesh, ye shall die: but if ye through the Spirit do mortify the deeds of the

body, ye shall live.

Our fleshly desires will always lead us astray. Our carnal nature must be crucified!

Galatians 5:24
And they that are Christ's have crucified the flesh with the affections and lusts.

In fact, this is the whole reason for the "new covenant." Keeping the law outwardly was not sufficient. Therefore, God said He would put the law in our hearts.

Jeremiah 31:33
But this shall be the covenant that I will make with the house of Israel; After those days, saith the LORD, I will put my law in their inward parts, and write it in their hearts; and will be their God, and they shall be my people.

2 Corinthians 3:3
Forasmuch as ye are manifestly declared to be the epistle of Christ ministered by us, written not with ink, but with the Spirit of the living God; not in tables of stone, but in fleshy tables of the heart.

When this transformation takes place, it will result in changes in our inner man which will be visible to others. We will cease producing "the works of the flesh" and begin producing something far better.

Galatians 5:22-23
But the fruit of the Spirit is love, joy, peace, longsuffering, gentleness, goodness, faith, ²³Meekness, temperance: against such there is no law.

"These are not gifts that we pray for or seek after. Through our personal consecration to God, we are gradually changed inwardly until these characteristics of His nature begin to be recognized outwardly in our lives. God's Spirit will challenge and change us inwardly as long as we willingly make the outward changes necessary to please Him."[17]

It is possible to look holy on the outside and be carnal on the inside! Consider the prodigal son's older brother, who, according to his own words, was never guilty of ANY of the "outward" sins and transgressions his brother committed.

> **Luke 15:29-30**
> *And he answering said to his father, Lo, these many years do I serve thee, neither transgressed I at any time thy commandment: and yet thou never gavest me a kid, that I might make merry with my friends: [30]But as soon as this thy son was come, which hath devoured thy living with harlots, thou hast killed for him the fatted calf.*

His personal testimony was, "Neither transgressed I at any time thy commandment." I doubt he would have said this to his father had it not been true.

Despite that fact, however, his spirit was filled with anger, jealousy, and – perhaps most glaringly of all – self-righteousness. He saw himself as far more "worthy" and "deserving" of reward than his repentant brother. If we are not careful, we can mark off our "checklist" of outward standards while allowing our spirit to be totally repulsive to God!

> **Isaiah 65:2-5**
> *I have spread out my hands all the day unto a rebellious people, which walketh in a way that was not good, after their own thoughts; [3]A people that provoketh me to anger continually to my*

---

[17] Stewart, Missionary Jessie, *Inward Holiness,* taught at a conference in the Republic of South Africa on March 28, 2024.

A Right Spirit

> *face; that sacrificeth in gardens, and burneth incense upon altars of brick; ⁴Which remain among the graves, and lodge in the monuments, which eat swine's flesh, and broth of abominable things is in their vessels; ⁵Which say, Stand by thyself, come not near to me; for I am holier than thou. These are a smoke in my nose, a fire that burneth all the day.*

The Contemporary English Version says, "Such people are like smoke, irritating my nose all day."[18] Regardless of how "holy" we look on the outside, we must never allow our spirits to be defiled by bitterness, envy, strife, greed, pride, "and such like."

I could write a separate chapter on each of these, but to do so would be beyond the scope of this volume. Suffice it to say we must obey Paul's admonition for both outward AND inward cleansing.

> **2 Corinthians 7:1**
>
> *Having therefore these promises, dearly beloved, let us cleanse ourselves from all filthiness of the flesh and spirit, perfecting holiness in the fear of God.*

It should be our daily practice to pray a prayer of daily repentance. One great example we can use as a guide is the prayer David penned after his sin with Bathsheba.

> **Psalms 51:10**
>
> *Create in me a clean heart, O God; and renew a right spirit within me.*

David recognized his sin had sprung from something deep within him. His issue was more than a physical lust – it was a

---

[18] *The Contemporary English Version*, Thomas Nelson Publishers, 1995.

problem in his spirit! He alluded to this in the very next verse.

Psalms 51:11
Cast me not away from thy presence; and take not thy holy spirit from me.

The *Darby Translation* reads, "Cast me not away from thy presence, and take not the spirit of thy holiness from me."[19] This is precisely WHY the "Holy Ghost" is not named for any other attribute of God – it is first and foremost a "spirit of holiness!"

Sin starts inside. It should be dealt with accordingly.

James 1:14-15
But every man is tempted, when he is drawn away of his own lust, and enticed. ¹⁵Then when lust hath conceived, it bringeth forth sin: and sin, when it is finished, bringeth forth death.

Sin is the result of the carnal desires which spring from our flesh and can only be controlled by a right spirit. For this reason, we must be "strengthened ... in the inner man."

Ephesians 3:16
That he would grant you, according to the riches of his glory, to be strengthened with might by his Spirit in the inner man;

When Paul prayed for the saints at Thessalonica, he expressed his desire for them. He wanted them to be "blameless" in every regard.

1 Thessalonians 5:23
And the very God of peace sanctify you wholly; and I pray God your whole spirit and soul and body be preserved blameless unto the coming of

---

[19] *The Holy Bible: Darby Translation;* Christian Classics Ethereal Library; 2002.

> our Lord Jesus Christ.

The International Standard Version says, "May the God of peace himself make you holy in every way. And may your whole being—spirit, soul, and body—remain blameless when our Lord Jesus, the Messiah, appears."[20] It is only when our body AND soul AND spirit are blameless that we can be considered "wholly sanctified" (i.e., "holy in every way") unto God. We must have the outward SIGNS of holiness and, more importantly, the inward SPIRIT of holiness!

Romans 1:4

> *And declared to be the Son of God with power, according to the spirit of holiness, by the resurrection from the dead:*

The "spirit of holiness" was the thing that declared Christ to be the Son of God. How much more, then, should WE (as sons and daughters of God) NEED that same spirit of holiness – not just the outward form, but the inward transformation – to make that declaration for us?

---

[20] *The Holy Bible: International Standard Version*, Davidson Press, 2003.

THE NEED FOR STANDARDS

Isaiah 59:19
So shall they fear the name of the Lord from the west, and his glory from the rising of the sun. When the enemy shall come in like a flood, the Spirit of the Lord shall lift up a standard against him.

As I have pointed out over the last few chapters, God expects His people to be separate from the rest of the world. If we are required to be separate, how do we determine whether we are truly separate? It should be evident that some "standards" must be set by which the world may observe our separation. It is essential that we do so.

Earlier in this book, I addressed a verse many use to deny the importance of separation. We want to look at this verse again, pointing out something I did not address last time.

1 Samuel 16:7
But the LORD said unto Samuel, Look not on his countenance, or on the height of his stature; because I have refused him: for the LORD seeth not as man seeth; for man looketh on the outward appearance, but the LORD looketh on the heart.

As I pointed out previously, this refers to choosing a king and has nothing to do with outward holiness. We know this because God mentioned "countenance" and "height of stature." He said NOTHING about clothing!

The Need for Standards

With this being said, however, something else needs to be noted. The Bible says, "Man looketh on the outward appearance." It is MEN whom we are trying to win to God, and they can ONLY see what is on the outside. Therefore, our outside MUST reflect to the world what is on the inside because man cannot see our heart. Thus, I again stress the fact that there MUST be some way we can observably show the world God has changed our lives. We do this when our outward appearance is governed by what we call "standards of holiness."

The word "standard" has several definitions. One is "something set up and established by authority as a rule for the measure of quantity, weight, extent, value, or quality."[21] For example, if there is no "standard" way to measure weight, a grocer could tell you he is selling a "pound" of meat, although it may be only a few ounces. Honest transactions require a consistent method of measurement. In other words, we need an accepted "standard".

Another definition is "something established by authority, custom, or general consent as a model or example."[22] This is how we use the word when speaking of "a standard of conduct." It denotes the criterion of excellence by which all others are judged.

To fully comprehend the word "standard," however, we need to consider the origins of the word. The Online Etymology Dictionary offers the following definition for the word "standard": "'Flag or other conspicuous object to serve as a rallying point for a military force,' from the shortened form of an Old French word, *estandart,* [which means] 'military standard, banner.'… [This is] probably from the Frankish *standhard, literally 'stand fast or firm'… so called because the flag was fixed to a pole or spear and

---

[21] Merriam-Webster Dictionary, https://www.merriam-webster.com/dictionary/standard

[22] *Ibid.*

stuck in the ground to stand upright."[23]

Thus, when we think of "standards," we should immediately think of a flag flown high for the whole world to notice. The word "flag" is defined as: "a piece of cloth, varying in size, shape, color, and design, usually attached at one edge to a staff or cord, and used as the symbol of a nation, state, or organization, as a means of signaling, etc.; ensign; standard; banner; pennant."[24]

The Biblical use of the word "standard" in connection with the concept of a flag is shown in the Book of Numbers. In the following verse, the Israelites were commanded to "pitch" (or set up their tents) by their "own standard" (or flag).

Numbers 2:2
Every man of the children of Israel shall pitch by his own standard, with the ensign of their father's house: far off about the tabernacle of the congregation shall they pitch.

The Israelites camped around the Tabernacle according to their tribes. Each tribe had a flag that bore the "standard" (or emblem) of his father's house. This was a visible sign which allowed everyone to know who their father was, which is precisely what "standards of holiness" do for us today. They tell the world Who our Father is!

Although they are often misunderstood (and sometimes even resented), standards of holiness can be of great value to the people of God. This is especially true when followed for the right purpose and in the right spirit.

Paul taught that the gifts of the Spirit were more beneficial when administered in love. (See I Corinthians 13). Similarly, standards will be more advantageous when we understand their

---

[23] Online Etymology Dictionary, https://www.etymonline.com

[24] Dictionary.com, https://www.dictionary.com/browse/flag

purpose and that they are administrated in love. The more the purpose and use of standards are understood, the better qualified a person will be to keep them.

I contend that people will be more likely to do things they understand. Although the people of God must trust their leadership regarding holiness standards, this trust will come much easier if they have a clear understanding of the reason behind the standard.

As I will explain later, there are times when the pastor can give no reason beyond what he feels in the Holy Ghost. Saints should accept this and willingly obey. Nevertheless, the overwhelming majority of standards have been set for a purpose – either there is a clear Biblical mandate, or there are Scriptural principles upon which the standards are established. Whichever is the case, the members of an assembly need to realize standards are not simply a way for the pastor to control someone's life. Instead, they are guidelines given by the pastor to help the members control their own lives!

David was called "a man after God's own heart." There were no doubt many reasons for this. Personally, I cannot help but believe one of those reasons was David's desire to clearly and openly identify with the One True God of Israel.

Psalm 20:5
> We will rejoice in thy salvation, and in the name of our God we will set up our banners: the Lord fulfil all thy petitions.

David proclaimed that his "banners" (i.e., flags) would be "set up" – not in his own name, but "in the name of our God." He chose to fly flags that physically identified him with the Lord to anyone who approached him. Those "standards" proudly proclaimed to all the world that David's trust, confidence, and strength came from Jehovah, and it would be Jehovah Who would fight for him!

Understanding Separation

Like David, we, too, should understand the purpose – and promise – of standards. Our outward holiness standards are a visible proclamation to everyone we meet that God is our Father and we are a part of His church.

During a war, brave soldiers who are not afraid of their enemy are willing to wave their nation's flag high. Perhaps one of the most iconic photos in American history is the raising of the flag on Iwo Jima – a statement to the enemy that the United States was victorious over a major Japanese outpost. History says this was actually the second U.S. flag to be put there, as the first one was considered too small to be seen well enough![25] The American troops wanted to be sure their comrades AND their enemies knew they had scaled – and taken – Mount Suribachi!

God's people should never be afraid (and certainly never ashamed) to hold a standard that provides a clear, unquestionable statement of the Lord's victory in our lives. We should lift the banner of holiness high, removing any and all doubt as to whose side we are on!

We are engaged in spiritual warfare. We must lift up the "standards" against the flood of wickedness that is rising up against the church.

The church is ordained to be a light in this world. Light stands out in the darkness. It causes the church to be conspicuous to the world. It is noticeable; it is obvious.

Matthew 5:14-16

Ye are the light of the world. A city that is set on an hill cannot be hid. ¹⁵Neither do men light a candle, and put it under a bushel, but on a candlestick; and it giveth light unto all that are in the house. ¹⁶Let your light so shine before men,

---

[25] Garner, Tom, Live Science, https://www.livescience.com/iwo-jima-flag-raising.html

that they may see your good works, and glorify your Father which is in heaven.

People need to see our outward efforts to please God. When they do, Jesus said it will cause them to glorify our Father. Our outward efforts identify Who our Father is!

That which attracts attention to a person is the light others see. Flamboyant clothing may draw attention to a person's flesh and cause others to misinterpret that person's spirit and true character. Similarly, modest clothing can control physical attraction toward an individual. This could reveal the Christian personality and allow the genuine character of that person to stand out.

The Apostle Paul gave Christians a unique designation. He said we are appointed to be the ambassadors of Jesus Christ.

2 Corinthians 5:20
Now then we are ambassadors for Christ, as though God did beseech you by us: we pray you in Christ's stead, be ye reconciled to God.

As ambassadors, we should reflect His light and glory to the world. It should be the church's objective to draw attention to the One Whom we represent rather than to ourselves. We should endeavor to be identified with Jesus Christ in every aspect of our lives. When properly applied to our lives, standards help bring this identity about.

Going back to our comparison between holiness standards and a flag or banner, we should recognize that nations, states, cities, and even organizations choose flags to represent certain customs and traditions that are important to them. Their flag is a visible symbol of the philosophy of life incorporated by the group flying the flag.

Generally speaking, at least two purposes are behind the design and/or colors chosen for the flag. One is to present the group's overarching principles and core beliefs in a positive (yet absolute) light. The other is to show any unique characteristics or qualities that allow the group to stand out among others.

For example, consider the United States Flag. It has 13 horizontal stripes – seven red and six white. In the upper left corner is a field of blue, which encases 50 white stars. According to the Continental Congress, which authorized the original flag, the 13 stripes represented the 13 original colonies. The stars were to represent the number of states. White signified purity and innocence, red represented hardiness and valor, and blue stood for vigilance, perseverance, and justice.[26]

With this idea of a flag representing distinct qualities, the concept of "standards" began to be applied to exemplary moral and spiritual baselines. Our holiness standards tell the world we are distinct in our lifestyle and unique in our relationship to God. In short, holiness standards are "flags" which are a visible testament to God's ownership of our lives.

The children of God should not look upon standards of holiness as something that makes us "homely" or "undesirable." While the world may see us that way, God sees our holiness of lifestyle in an entirely different manner.

> ***Psalm 149:4***
> *For the Lord taketh pleasure in his people: he will beautify the meek with salvation.*
>
> ***Psalms 29:2***
> *Give unto the LORD the glory due unto his name; worship the LORD in the beauty of holiness.*

To God, there is nothing "ugly" about the holiness of His people. To Him, it is a matter of great beauty!

---

[26] PBS, *The History of the American Flag*, https://www.pbs.org/a-capitol-fourth/history/old-glory

The Need for Standards

There are at least four things holiness standards represent in our lives. First and foremost, they represent ***distinction***.

Make no mistake. God has always required His people to be different from every other people on earth.

> ***2 Corinthians 6:14-18***
>
> *Be ye not unequally yoked together with unbelievers: for what fellowship hath righteousness with unrighteousness? and what communion hath light with darkness? [15]And what concord hath Christ with Belial? or what part hath he that believeth with an infidel? [16]And what agreement hath the temple of God with idols? for ye are the temple of the living God; as God hath said, I will dwell in them, and walk in them; and I will be their God, and they shall be my people. [17]Wherefore come out from among them, and be ye separate, saith the Lord, and touch not the unclean thing; and I will receive you, [18]And will be a Father unto you, and ye shall be my sons and daughters, saith the Lord Almighty.*

God expects distinction. The devil, on the other hand, does his best to get the church to compromise. He desires to blur the lines between the church and the world.

Part of this process is to blur the lines between the genders. The Bible is clear that God created only two genders – male and female – and He has always expected the two to be distinct in their actions and their appearance. (This will be dealt with in more detail later in this book.)

Today's society is doing all it can to convince us there is no difference between men and women while at the same time saying people should be able to "change" from one gender to another. My question is simple: If there's no difference, why is there a need to change?

All of this is nothing more than an attempt to remove distinction and separation. It began with a blurring of the lines with regard to clothing. It has now reached a point where there is no longer a line to blur!

This cannot be the case in the church of the Living God. Our standards of holiness help to set us apart from the rest of the world. As a result of having been converted, we should look different, dress different, act different, think different, and BE different – in EVERY way!

Both in the manner of dress and in codes of conduct, the church is different from the world. That distinction and difference is very pleasing to God. To God, our beauty is not in physical features but rather in the spirit and character of the inner man. How beautiful it is to have God's Spirit radiating from our lives!

Psalm 149:4
For the LORD taketh pleasure in his people: he will beautify the meek with salvation.

Standards of holiness don't only serve the purpose of providing a clear distinction between the church and the world. They serve other purposes as well.

Standards also represent ***a declaration of war.*** They are our military ensigns or flags. Although the enemy is coming against us in a flood of immorality, humanism, perversion, divorce, and abortion, the church should not sit idle and passive. The standard must be lifted as our military ensign against the attack of the enemy.

Isaiah 59:19
So shall they fear the name of the Lord from the west, and his glory from the rising of the sun. When the enemy shall come in like a flood, the Spirit of the Lord shall lift up a standard against him.

The Need for Standards

Although the world of sin may become darker, it will only make the light and truth of the church more obvious. There will always be a people who will stand for righteousness in the face of adversity. They will not be afraid to raise high the standard of the church.

The Bible is FILLED with examples of individuals who were banners of truth and righteousness! For example, what a banner for righteousness Joshua and Caleb were as they stood before the entire camp of the Israelites! What a banner the three Hebrews were in the fiery furnace! David stood alone before Goliath; Noah stood alone by his ark; Abraham stood alone with his promise; and Joseph stood alone with his dream. All of these were "banners of truth" waving high before the world.

Standards also represent *quality.* The church is a spectacle to the world. Life is like a theater stage upon which we pass but once. Christians are on display, showing the quality of life God has given us. If for no other reason, we should display high standards to reveal the value of God's work in us. He has truly made something beautiful of our lives.

Romans 8:15

For ye have not received the spirit of bondage again to fear; but ye have received the Spirit of adoption, whereby we cry, Abba, Father.

1 Peter 2:9

But ye are a chosen generation, a royal priesthood, an holy nation, a peculiar people; that ye should shew forth the praises of him who hath called you out of darkness into his marvellous light:

God has adopted us into His royal family. Because of this relationship, we have an obligation to live based on higher principles than those around us.

It has been said that a young princess of England was once being directed by her governess to discipline herself. The child said, "I do not have to do that; I am the princess." The governess wisely replied, "That is exactly why you must do it."

Since we are the royalty of God, we should gladly bear the standards of the royal family. Through this, we allow the world to see not only our distinction and separation but also the high quality of life that our Father has given us.

Everything God does in a person's life is for his good. It is for the purpose of transforming us into His character.

> ***Romans 8:28-29***
>
> *And we know that all things work together for good to them that love God, to them who are the called according to his purpose. ²⁹For whom he did foreknow, he also did predestinate to be conformed to the image of his Son, that he might be the firstborn among many brethren.*

God desires to see the highest quality produced in the Christian life. The standard of quality is apparent through a Christian's life and character. The standards set by the Christian are to be reflective of the high standard of quality he desires in his life.

Standards represent ***ownership and conquest.*** As explorers landed on new and distant shores, one of the first things they would do was to plant a flag to show the kingdom they represented was claiming this territory as their own. When man landed on the moon, what did Neil Armstrong do? He planted a flag!

We are not our own. Because we belong to God, we should gladly show Who has taken control of our lives!

> ***1 Corinthians 6:19-20***
>
> *What? know ye not that your body is the temple of the Holy Ghost which is in you, which ye have*

of God, and ye are not your own? ^{20}For ye are bought with a price: therefore glorify God in your body, and in your spirit, which are God's.

Standards represent *a united effort.* We are part of something bigger than ourselves. We should be willing to show that we identify with others of "like precious faith."

Psalm 133:1
Behold, how good and how pleasant it is for brethren to dwell together in unity!

Uniforms create a specific identity. Every policeman wears a uniform that looks like all the others worn by the people on that same force. All the United States postmen have a familiar dress. Each time you see this kind of uniformed person, he represents one of many. His clothing speaks of a united effort to distribute mail or control the crime and violence of the city.

By the same token, the Christian should have in his lifestyle, his philosophy of life, his character, and even standards of dress something that speaks of the united effort of the church to live for God. This does not mean all Christians should wear the same uniform. It does mean, however, that certain characteristics of the standards of the church cause the world to recognize us as belonging to Jesus Christ.

A united endeavor cannot exist without discipline, direction, order, and authority. Today, many do what is right in their own eyes. Many are dishonest and willfully break the law. A rebellious generation without a moral code is dominating our society. The church should see this as a call to arise and show the standard of right direction and order. We must produce the fruit of a disciplined life and allow the adhesiveness of authority to unify us in our stand for that which is right.

A united effort can be maintained only through submission to authority as established in Scripture. The Bible teaches submission to parents (Ephesians 6:1-3), to employers (Ephesians 6:5-8), to the government (Romans 13:1-7), and to church leaders (Hebrews 13:17).

God's distinct reference to obedience (I Samuel 15:22-23) and His stern action against the rebellious (Numbers 16:31-35) reveal His standard of submission to authority. The purpose of submission is to keep the united work of the church operating.

The last thing we should know is that standards are an essential form of *protection*. Many years ago, in the American West, every major ranch had fences built around their perimeters. These fences served one primary purpose – they were there for the protection of their inhabitants.

This protection, however, worked two ways. The fences kept the enemy (rustlers, wild animals, etc.) out. They also guarded the populace within, keeping them from roaming to dangerous places where they did not belong.

Standards do the same thing for us. They keep the enemy out by establishing guidelines that "give no place for the devil."

> **Ephesians 4:27**
> *Neither give place to the devil.*

They also keep the populace from roaming to "dangerous places" by establishing guidelines that are a safe distance from harm. Furthermore, standards not only protect us, they protect the glory of God!

> **Isaiah 6:3-4**
> *And one cried unto another, and said, Holy, holy, holy, is the LORD of hosts: the whole earth is full of his glory. ⁴And the posts of the door moved at the voice of him that cried, and the house was filled with smoke.*

One significant thing to notice about what took place in this passage is that things didn't start "moving" in the House of God

The Need for Standards

until there was an open proclamation of God's Holiness! Once the messengers began crying, "Holy, holy, holy," the posts moved, and the glory filled the house!

> **2 Corinthians 6:17-18**
> *Wherefore come out from among them, and be ye separate, saith the Lord, and touch not the unclean thing; and I will receive you, ^{18}And will be a Father unto you, and ye shall be my sons and daughters, saith the Lord Almighty.*

Paul emphatically stated we only have God's promise of paternity as long as we maintain a passion for purity! If we don't bear a resemblance to God's holiness, we cannot rightfully claim to be His children.

> **1 John 2:15**
> *Love not the world, neither the things that are in the world. If any man love the world, the love of the Father is not in him.*

This is a profound statement. If a love for the world is present in us, it reveals an absence of the love of God.

> **Romans 5:5**
> *And hope maketh not ashamed; because the love of God is shed abroad in our hearts by the Holy Ghost which is given unto us.*

If God's love is absent, that, too, is an indicator of a problem. If we lack the love of God, we are lacking the Spirit of God!

The more full of the Holy Ghost we become, the more we love God. The more we love God, the less we love the things of the world. The less we love the things of the world, the more we recognize God's paternity in our lives. The more we recognize His position over us, the more we proclaim His holiness. The more we proclaim His holiness, the more we have a move of the Spirit. In short, we maintain standards not just to keep the devil out but to keep God in – and to keep Him moving and working in our lives!

In the late 1800's, a poet by the name of Joseph Malins wrote a poem that illustrates the important of fences. I know of no better way to close this chapter (and thereby stress the important of having holiness standards) than to share this poem.

"*A Fence or an Ambulance*"

By Joseph Malins

'Twas a dangerous cliff, as they freely confessed,
Though to walk near its crest was so pleasant;
But over its terrible edge there had slipped
A duke and full many a peasant.
So the people said something would have to be done,
But here projects did not at all tally.
Some said, "Put up a fence around the edge of the cliff,"
Some, "An ambulance down in the valley."

But the cry for the ambulance carried the day,
For it spread through the neighboring city.
A fence may be useful or not, it is true,
But each heart became full of pity
For those who slipped over that dangerous cliff;
And dwellers in highway and alley
Gave pounds or gave pence, not to put up a fence,
But an ambulance down in the valley.

The Need for Standards

"For a cliff is all right, if you're careful," they said,
"And if folks even slip and are dropping,
It isn't the slipping that hurts them so much,
As the shock down below when they're stopping."
So day after day, as the mishaps occurred,
Quick forth would these rescuers sally
To pick up the victims who fell off the cliff,
With their ambulance down in the valley.

Then an old sage remarked, "It's a marvel to me
That people give more attention
to repairing results than to stopping the cause,
When they'd much better aim at prevention.
Let's stop at its source all this mischief," cried he,
"Come, neighbors and friends, let us rally!
If the cliff we will fence, we might also dispense
With the ambulance down in the valley."

"Oh he's a fanatic," the others rejoined,
"Dispense with the ambulance? Never!
He'd dispense with all charities, too, if he could;
No! No! We'll support them forever.
Aren't we picking up folks just as fast as they fall?
And shall this man dictate to us? Shall he?
Why should people of sense stop to put up a fence,
While the ambulance works in the valley?"

> But a sensible few, who are practical too,
> Will not bear with such nonsense much longer.
> They believe that prevention is better than cure,
> And their party will soon be the stronger.
> Encourage them then with your purse, voice, and pen,
> And while other philanthropists dally,
> They will scorn all pretense and put up a stout fence
> On the cliff that hangs over the valley.
>
> Better guide well the young than reclaim them when old,
> For the voice of true wisdom is calling,
> "To rescue the fallen is good, 'But tis best
> To prevent other people from falling."
> Better close up the source of temptation and crime
> Than deliver from dungeon or galley.
> Better put a strong fence around the top of the cliff,
> Than an ambulance down in the valley.[27]

---

[27] Malins, Joseph, *A Fence or an Ambulance*, 1895 or 1898 (sources uncertain), printed in the Iowa Health Bulletin in 1912.

The Need for Standards

LIFTING A STANDARD

Isaiah 59:19
So shall they fear the name of the LORD from the west, and his glory from the rising of the sun. When the enemy shall come in like a flood, the Spirit of the LORD shall lift up a standard against him.

In the previous chapter, I pointed out God's command for separation, the importance of distinction, and the significance of what holiness standards represent. In this chapter, I want to help you understand the sources from which those standards originate.

If set arbitrarily, standards can cause confusion and division in the body of Christ. Of course, such confusion does NOT come from God.

1 Corinthians 14:33
For God is not the author of confusion, but of peace, as in all churches of the saints.

In such cases, sincere people who desire to conform to the right models and ideals of the church can be hurt and lose their direction. Understanding how we set standards will help avoid such confusion. Therefore, I want to show you six principles for establishing godly standards of holiness.

First and foremost, **the Word of God sets standards**. After all, the Word of God is the expression of the mind of God. It conveys to us God's will for all humanity and reveals the history of how God deals with humanity.

When we know how God thinks concerning the issues of life, we should have little doubt about His standards. This knowledge of God's will through His Word is a great treasure to the Christian.

Understanding the principles established in His Word helps to define many of the church's standards because they are clearly indicated in the Bible. Others must be interpreted by adequately understanding God's principles and rightly dividing the Word of Truth. The more we apply ourselves to diligent study of the Bible, the more we may understand and appreciate the standards God has set for His people.

We should note how often the Bible connects our love for God with doing the things written in His Word. Here are just a few of many examples.

John 14:15
If ye love me, keep my commandments.

John 14:21
He that hath my commandments, and keepeth them, he it is that loveth me: and he that loveth me shall be loved of my Father, and I will love him, and will manifest myself to him.

John 14:23-24
Jesus answered and said unto him, If a man love me, he will keep my words: and my Father will love him, and we will come unto him, and make our abode with him. [24]He that loveth me not keepeth not my sayings: and the word which ye hear is not mine, but the Father's which sent me.

1 John 3:10
In this the children of God are manifest, and the children of the devil: whosoever doeth not

> *righteousness is not of God, neither he that loveth not his brother.*

> **1 John 3:24**
> *And he that keepeth his commandments dwelleth in him, and he in him. And hereby we know that he abideth in us, by the Spirit which he hath given us.*

I mentioned that I plan to list six ways standards are set. However, it is essential to note that NONE of the remaining ways can contradict, violate, or supersede the first one! If the Word of God sets a standard, it is forever settled!

> **Psalms 119:89**
> *For ever, O LORD, thy word is settled in heaven.*

Second, **the Spirit of God sets standards.** At times, we may not understand what the Bible teaches about certain modern technologies and/or philosophies. In such cases, the Spirit will often quicken our minds to certain verses of Scripture or reveal certain things as harmful to our spiritual well-being. These times of prompting by the Spirit are referred to as conviction.

When the Pentecostal movement first began in North America many years ago, people did not know tobacco caused cancer. Still, there were many who felt convicted by the Spirit that it was wrong to use tobacco in any form, even though the use of tobacco is not dealt with directly by the Bible. Only recently was it proven that this substance is harmful and addictive to the body, but God had convicted His people about it many years before anyone realized that fact.

God dealt with His people in a similar fashion concerning television. It looked like a promising tool of communication when it first emerged, and much of the programming at the time could not be proven to be harmful. But God knew how it would rapidly deteriorate into one the most influential tools the devil has yet used. Many people felt a conviction against television by the Spirit when it was first introduced. It is obvious today, even to the secular world, that it has been a bad influence on our society. For years, many people were ridiculed by the world for being against television. Now, some of those who embraced television are beginning to fight against it as they, too, see its harmful influence.

There are times when the Spirit convicts people concerning certain practices because He knows the end result of it. They are sensitive to God and realize a need to conform to the conviction of their hearts. Even if we do not share their conviction, we must be careful not to dismiss it lightly or think less of the individual. It is always good to respect the convictions of others.

> **Romans 8:14**
> *For as many as are led by the Spirit of God, they are the sons of God.*
>
> **Galatians 5:16**
> *This I say then, Walk in the Spirit, and ye shall not fulfil the lust of the flesh.*
>
> **Galatians 5:25**
> *If we live in the Spirit, let us also walk in the Spirit.*

The third method of establishing holiness standards is when **the man of God sets standards.** As proof, consider the example of Moses and the Children of Israel.

> **Exodus 19:12-13**
> *And thou shalt set bounds unto the people round about, saying, Take heed to yourselves, that ye go not up into the mount, or touch the border of it: whosoever toucheth the mount shall be surely put to death: 13There shall not an hand touch it, but he shall surely be stoned, or shot*

through; whether it be beast or man, it shall not live: when the trumpet soundeth long, they shall come up to the mount.

There are two things you should notice about this passage. First, God said there were some places you just should not go!

Second, God left it up to Moses to determine where the "bounds" would be. How do you decide where a mountain starts? They don't generally come up out of the ground at a 45° angle. Rather, they gradually slope upwards. Finding the exact spot where a mountain starts rising would obviously be a difficult task.

Nevertheless, God said anyone who touched the mountain was to be put to death. It was left up to Moses to decide what was "safe" territory for those following him.

In the same way, pastors today have to be granted the liberty to decide the boundaries (*i.e.,* the standards) for the assembly God has placed under his watch. In no case is he permitted to violate what the Word of God has settled, of course, but anything not explicitly stated in the Scripture falls within his purview of authority.

Hebrews 13:17

Obey them that have the rule over you, and submit yourselves: for they watch for your souls, as they that must give account, that they may do it with joy, and not with grief: for that is unprofitable for you.

The man of God has to give an account for your soul. He will answer for what he has preached and what he has not preached.

Ezekiel 33:1-9

Again the word of the LORD came unto me, saying, ²Son of man, speak to the children of thy people, and say unto them, When I bring the sword upon a land, if the people of the land take a man of their coasts, and set him for their watchman: ³If when he seeth the sword come upon the land, he blow the trumpet, and warn the people; ⁴Then whosoever heareth the sound of the trumpet, and taketh not warning; if the sword come, and take him away, his blood shall be upon his own head. ⁵He heard the sound of the trumpet, and took not warning; his blood shall be upon him. But he that taketh warning shall deliver his soul. ⁶But if the watchman see the sword come, and blow not the trumpet, and the people be not warned; if the sword come, and take any person from among them, he is taken away in his iniquity; but his blood will I require at the watchman's hand. ⁷So thou, O son of man, I have set thee a watchman unto the house of Israel; therefore thou shalt hear the word at my mouth, and warn them from me. ⁸When I say unto the wicked, O wicked man, thou shalt surely die; if thou dost not speak to warn the wicked from his way, that wicked man shall die in his iniquity; but his blood will I require at thine hand. ⁹Nevertheless, if thou warn the wicked of his way to turn from it; if he do not turn from his way, he shall die in his iniquity; but thou hast delivered thy soul.

The Apostle Paul issued a grave warning to the watchman. He instructed them to "take heed" to the flock, reminding them the very blood of Christ purchased these people!

Acts 20:28
Take heed therefore unto yourselves, and to all

> *the flock, over the which the Holy Ghost hath made you overseers, to feed the church of God, which he hath purchased with his own blood.*

Likewise, the Apostle Peter sternly exhorted the men of God as to how they handled the saints entrusted to them. He wanted them to always keep in mind that these precious people were God's flock and should be treated accordingly.

> ***1 Peter 5:1-3***
> *The elders which are among you I exhort, who am also an elder, and a witness of the sufferings of Christ, and also a partaker of the glory that shall be revealed: ²Feed the flock of God which is among you, taking the oversight thereof, not by constraint, but willingly; not for filthy lucre, but of a ready mind; ³Neither as being lords over God's heritage, but being ensamples to the flock.*

Since he understands these principles, it is with great care and caution that your pastor watches for your soul. Because he has the oversight of the flock, he will lovingly and prayerfully set standards for his congregation.

A pastor knows his people. He knows what things they can handle and what things would become a stumbling block to them. Therefore, he must have the ability to set standards within the local assembly.

This is why saints should not question (or judge) when visiting another assembly with slightly different standards than the church they attend. They should understand that God placed them under a godly, caring watchman who understands what is best for them. Another godly man may set the boundaries at a different location because he knows his flock and every congregation is different.

This is NOT to say, of course, that a pastor can ignore the CLEAR boundaries established by the Bible. I'm talking about things that are NOT specifically stated in Scriptural precepts. For example, one pastor may set a sleeve length somewhere between the elbow and wrist, while another puts it TO the wrist. Is one wrong and the other right? NO! As we will discuss in another chapter, the Biblical standard is "modest," and the local pastor is given the liberty to determine where that line of modesty is (within certain parameters that will be defined later).

The thing to remember is we are not in competition with another church. We are not even supposed to be making comparisons with other churches! (See 2 Corinthians 10:12.)

The next method of setting standards may come as a shock to some, but it is true nonetheless. **Tradition sets standards.**

While many people who have departed from formal denominations fear tradition, many traditions are good to keep. We know this based on Paul's writings.

2 Thessalonians 2:15
Therefore, brethren, stand fast, and hold the traditions which ye have been taught, whether by word, or our epistle.

In this verse, Paul admonished Christians to "hold the traditions which ye have been taught." He reiterated this in the very next chapter.

2 Thessalonians 3:6
Now we command you, brethren, in the name of our Lord Jesus Christ, that ye withdraw yourselves from every brother that walketh disorderly, and not after the tradition which he received of us.

Here, he taught them to "withdraw" from those who refused to follow the godly traditions handed to them by their elders. The great apostle knew these traditions had not been created indiscriminately but prayerfully. The elders had a reason for the things they established, and those guidelines should not be quickly relinquished.

Not only did Paul say these things to the church in Thessalonica. He also wrote something very similar to Corinth.

> *1 Corinthians 11:2*
> *Now I praise you, brethren, that ye remember me in all things, and keep the ordinances, as I delivered them to you.*

He praised the Corinthians for keeping the ordinances (literally, traditions) as he had delivered them. *The English Standard Version* reads, "Now I commend you because you remember me in everything and maintain the traditions even as I delivered them to you."[28] *God's Word Translation* says, "I praise you for always thinking about me and for carefully following the traditions that I handed down to you."[29]

Remember that the church in Corinth was filled with problems that the apostle had to address. These ranged from "cliques" (chapters 1-3), to immorality (chapter 5), to disbelief concerning the resurrection of the dead (chapter 15), and much more! In spite of this, he said there was one thing for which he commended them. That one thing was they held on to the traditions he had established among them.

Daniel would not eat the king's meat because it was a lawful tradition in Israel not to eat meat offered to idols. The Rechabites would drink no wine because it was a tradition in their family.

> *Jeremiah 35:14*
> *The words of Jonadab the son of Rechab, that he commanded his sons not to drink wine, are performed; for unto this day they drink none, but*

---

[28] *The Holy Bible: English Standard Version,* Crossway Books, 2001.

[29] *God's Word Translation,* Baker Books, 2010.

> *obey their father's commandment: notwithstanding I have spoken unto you, rising early and speaking; but ye hearkened not unto me.*

God used this to condemn Israel because these people were more strict in keeping their family tradition than the nation of Israel was in keeping the precepts of God.

Some standards may be set in the church that are not specifically dealt with in the Scriptures, but they have been long-standing traditions. We should not be quick to discredit such traditional standards. Remember that much time, consideration, and prayer have usually gone into the decision to take such a stand. These traditions are generally built on the foundation of some principle of God and should not be considered lightly.

> ***Proverbs 11:14***
> *Where no counsel is, the people fall: but in the multitude of counsellors there is safety.*

There is safety in the multitude of godly counsellors. It is wise to revere and respect standards that have become long-standing traditions.

Another method of establishing standards is that **culture sets standards.** For example, in some cultures, the lighting of a candle in church speaks of praying for the dead. In those areas, it would be inappropriate to have a candlelight service. Those who had come from this cultural background would be confused and might be tempted to start praying for their dead once again.

Paul dealt with these same problems with regard to eating meat offered to idols in both his first letter to the Corinthians and his letter to the Romans. In these passages, he pointed out the culture itself dictated certain standards that the church had to set in order to stay above reproach.

> ***1 Corinthians 8:4***
> *As concerning therefore the eating of those*

things that are offered in sacrifice unto idols, we know that an idol is nothing in the world, and that there is none other God but one.

1 Corinthians 8:7-12
Howbeit there is not in every man that knowledge: for some with conscience of the idol unto this hour eat it as a thing offered unto an idol; and their conscience being weak is defiled. ⁸But meat commendeth us not to God: for neither, if we eat, are we the better; neither, if we eat not, are we the worse. ⁹But take heed lest by any means this liberty of yours become a stumblingblock to them that are weak. ¹⁰For if any man see thee which hast knowledge sit at meat in the idol's temple, shall not the conscience of him which is weak be emboldened to eat those things which are offered to idols; ¹¹And through thy knowledge shall the weak brother perish, for whom Christ died? ¹²But when ye sin so against the brethren, and wound their weak conscience, ye sin against Christ.

Romans 14:7
For none of us liveth to himself, and no man dieth to himself.

Romans 14:10
But why dost thou judge thy brother? or why dost thou set at nought thy brother? for we shall all stand before the judgment seat of Christ.

We face the same problems in our day. Certain undesirable groups and lifestyles are often associated with a particular dress code, hairstyle, or behavior. When this occurs in any culture, the only way to avoid being identified with that group is to avoid the elements that mark them. In avoiding this identification, certain cultural standards become apparent.

The final way standards of holiness are established is when **the individual sets standards.** This does NOT mean you have the right (nor authority) to set your own standards that violate standards set through the other methods. This method is reserved for things NOT addressed by the other methods.

Every Christian should have certain convictions that fit his own life. Some people have found themselves craving certain things, such as coffee or soft drinks. They felt they should not allow such things to control their lives and laid them aside in self-discipline. While this is commendable, they should not expect everyone else to adopt their personal standard.

It is improper to impose our standards upon everyone else. Furthermore, ridiculing another man's convictions (or the lack thereof) is unkind and unchristian.

1 Corinthians 8:13
Wherefore, if meat make my brother to offend, I will eat no flesh while the world standeth, lest I make my brother to offend.

We must learn to respect the individual standards our brothers and sisters in the Lord have set for themselves. Never try to dissuade or discourage them from pursuing genuine God-given convictions.

When it comes to setting individual standards, let us thoroughly examine what we consider to be our convictions. As we do so, we must determine what the Spirit has dealt with us about. We must be honest. We must consider what effect it will have upon our fellow Christians. We must determine whether God or we ourselves will get the glory. Will the standard make us more spiritual and useful? If it does, by all means, live up to it.

Having set forth the ways standards are set, I believe it would be good to use the remainder of this chapter to summarize the reasons why standards are important in our lives. This knowledge should help us appreciate holiness standards – or, at the very least, keep us from resenting them.

Holiness standards show the world that God is working in the world. For Noah, that standard was building an ark and preaching righteousness. His faith condemned the world, and he became heir of that righteousness which is by faith.

Holiness standards point men to Christ. They show the world that we are God's children – God's unique people – Whose holiness has been imparted to us.

On the other hand, they are harmful if they merely point to a "holier-than-thou" attitude. As has already been said, God hates that attitude!

Isaiah 65:5

Which say, Stand by thyself, come not near to me; for I am holier than thou. These are a smoke in my nose, a fire that burneth all the day.

Matthew 23:1-7

Then spake Jesus to the multitude, and to his disciples, ²Saying, The scribes and the Pharisees sit in Moses' seat: ³All therefore whatsoever they bid you observe, that observe and do; but do not ye after their works: for they say, and do not. ⁴For they bind heavy burdens and grievous to be borne, and lay them on men's shoulders; but they themselves will not move them with one of their fingers. ⁵But all their works they do for to be seen of men: they make broad their phylacteries, and enlarge the borders of their garments, ⁶And love the uppermost rooms at feasts, and the chief seats

> in the synagogues, ⁷And greetings in the markets, and to be called of men, Rabbi, Rabbi.

Christ openly rebuked the Pharisees for their superficial standards. Standards are not an end in themselves. When that becomes the case, we become guilty of the world's charge of legalism. We are not to be legalistic.

Standards do not save us. Nevertheless, the lack of them will condemn us!

Hebrews 12:14
> Follow peace with all men, and holiness, without which no man shall see the Lord:

Holiness standards are tools to draw attention to the right things. They give direction and order to our lives and help us live a life that will help us be saved.

Let us maintain a proper attitude toward the purpose of standards. When we do, we will have a greater appreciation for them.

Holiness standards do not just serve as a fence, keeping us out of the world, but they are also the "guardian fences" of God, keeping the world out of us. They help protect us from the enemies of our souls, allowing us to live a more peaceful and quality life in the Spirit of God. Only then can we truly learn how to enjoy the abundant life brought to us by Jesus Christ.

.

PRESENT YOUR BODIES

1 Corinthians 3:16-17
Know ye not that ye are the temple of God, and that the Spirit of God dwelleth in you? [17]If any man defile the temple of God, him shall God destroy; for the temple of God is holy, which temple ye are.

A considerable portion of the first five books of the Bible contains explicit instructions concerning the proper use of the Tabernacle. If there is one message reiterated throughout those books, it is that the House of God was holy. As such, it was to be shown reverence, respect, and the utmost care.

Furthermore, when the Philistines took possession of the Ark of the Covenant (which belonged in the Tabernacle), they found themselves continually plagued with unusual and deadly diseases. (See 1 Samuel 6.) When Uzzah touched the ark, he fell dead. (See 2 Samuel 6.) When Belshazzar drank from the holy vessels, he sealed his fate, and the pronouncement of his judgment was written for all to see. (See Daniel 5.)

All of these facts serve as examples of the truth that God will not allow the abuse of holy things. Thus, when our bodies have been made holy by the indwelling presence of God, the Lord is definitely concerned about how we treat them.

1 Corinthians 3:16-17
Know ye not that ye are the temple of God, and that the Spirit of God dwelleth in you? [17]If any man defile the temple of God, him shall God destroy; for the temple of God is holy, which temple ye are.

Paul told the Corinthians that Christians are God's temple. He went on to say more specifically it is your body which is the temple of the Holy Ghost.

> **1 Corinthians 6:19-20**
>
> *What? know ye not that your body is the temple of the Holy Ghost which is in you, which ye have of God, and ye are not your own? [20]For ye are bought with a price: therefore glorify God in your body, and in your spirit, which are God's.*

We should glorify God in our bodies and in our spirits, which belong to God and are reserved for His holy purposes. This truth is so vital to God that He promised to destroy any who defile His temple.

Every sincere Christian should ask himself the following questions: "In what ways is it possible to defile my body? What steps of action can I take to purify the temple? Is defiling the temple purely a spiritual matter, or is it possible for the temple to be defiled by physical actions?"

The scope of the Apostle Paul's words in 1 Corinthians chapter six is that the temple is defiled by moral impurity. While the root of moral impurity is a spiritual matter, it is ultimately expressed by the body. Paul said that a person who commits fornication with a harlot becomes one flesh with the harlot.

> **1 Corinthians 6:15-18**
>
> *Know ye not that your bodies are the members of Christ? shall I then take the members of Christ, and make them the members of an harlot? God forbid. [16]What? know ye not that he which is joined to an harlot is one body? for two, saith he, shall be one flesh. [17]But he that is joined unto the Lord is one spirit. [18]Flee fornication. Every sin that a man doeth is without the body; but he that committeth fornication sinneth against his own body.*

The principle is that defilement begins in the spirit, but its final manifestation will be in the flesh. There is filthiness of the flesh *and* the spirit, and we are to cleanse ourselves from both.

> ***2 Corinthians 7:1***
>
> *Having therefore these promises, dearly beloved, let us cleanse ourselves from all filthiness of the flesh and spirit, perfecting holiness in the fear of God.*

What should be the attitude of the Christian toward fleshly sins like drinking, smoking, and drug abuse (among other things)? Are these purely physical matters, or do spiritual sins give birth to them?

> ***Mark 7:20-23***
>
> *And he said, That which cometh out of the man, that defileth the man. [21]For from within, out of the heart of men, proceed evil thoughts, adulteries, fornications, murders, [22]Thefts, covetousness, wickedness, deceit, lasciviousness, an evil eye, blasphemy, pride, foolishness: [23]All these evil things come from within, and defile the man.*

It is clear from Scripture that sin must have a body through which to express itself. This occurs as the members of the body are yielded to sinful practices.

> ***Romans 6:12-13***
>
> *Let not sin therefore reign in your mortal body, that ye should obey it in the lusts thereof. [13]Neither yield ye your members as instruments of unrighteousness unto sin: but yield yourselves unto God, as those that are alive from the dead, and your members as instruments of righteousness unto God.*

> ***Romans 6:16***
>
> *Know ye not, that to whom ye yield yourselves servants to obey, his servants ye are to whom ye obey; whether of sin unto death, or of obedience unto righteousness?*

It is, then, possible to sin with the body. Sinning is not just a matter of wrong attitudes or thoughts, although they are included. Sin can be committed with the eyes, ears, hands, feet, mind, mouth, or any other member of the body.

Jesus recognized the devastating effects of sins accomplished by body members. He boldly announced it would be better to be deprived of a hand, a foot, or an eye than to suffer the eternal fires of hell.

Mark 9:43-48

And if thy hand offend thee, cut it off: it is better for thee to enter into life maimed, than having two hands to go into hell, into the fire that never shall be quenched: [44]Where their worm dieth not, and the fire is not quenched. [45]And if thy foot offend thee, cut it off: it is better for thee to enter halt into life, than having two feet to be cast into hell, into the fire that never shall be quenched: [46]Where their worm dieth not, and the fire is not quenched. [47]And if thine eye offend thee, pluck it out: it is better for thee to enter into the kingdom of God with one eye, than having two eyes to be cast into hell fire: [48]Where their worm dieth not, and the fire is not quenched.

Christians should examine their physical habits to be sure they are not engaging in sinful practices. Since it is possible to sin with the body, and since the body of the believer is the temple of God, we must cleanse ourselves from the filthiness of the flesh according to God's command.

Over the next several pages, I want to deal with some specific areas of concern. These are not the only areas, but they are some of the most common.

- **Drinking**

    ### Proverbs 20:1

    Wine is a mocker, strong drink is raging: and whosoever is deceived thereby is not wise.

There are three categories of references to wine or drinking in Scripture. In some places where wine is mentioned, it is neither endorsed nor condemned. At other times, it is identified as a source of misery and/or as an emblem of the wrath of God. There are also passages where wine is portrayed as a blessing in conjunction with things like corn and bread.

Some religious movements today permit (or even encourage) the use of intoxicants in moderation. A careful examination of Scripture will reveal, however, that drinking alcoholic beverages is never spoken of favorably, and partaking of such beverages in any quantity is harmful to the human body. Intoxicants poison or fill the body with toxins. The intentional poisoning of our body is abusive to the temple of God. For these reasons, drinking is certainly a sinful practice in God's eyes, even when done in moderation.

Those references to wine falling under the first category mentioned cannot be used to support drinking. Scripture often mentions practices without condemning or condoning them as part of a larger context of mentioning human actions.

The references in the second category clearly condemn the use of wine in any quantity. One such denunciation of wine was written by Solomon, whom God had blessed with great wisdom.

Proverbs 23:29-35
Who hath woe? who hath sorrow? who hath contentions? who hath babbling? who hath wounds without cause? who hath redness of eyes? ^{30}They that tarry long at the wine; they that go to seek mixed wine. ^{31}Look not thou upon the wine when it is red, when it giveth his colour in the cup, when it moveth itself aright. ^{32}At the last it biteth like a serpent, and stingeth like an adder. ^{33}Thine eyes shall behold strange women, and thine heart shall utter perverse things. ^{34}Yea, thou shalt be as he that lieth down in the midst of the sea, or as he that lieth upon the top of a mast.

> ³⁵*They have stricken me, shalt thou say, and I was not sick; they have beaten me, and I felt it not: when shall I awake? I will seek it yet again.*

This passage graphically describes the evils of drinking intoxicating beverages. The sure result is sorrow, woe, contention, lust, senseless talk, and wounds. Drinking alcohol produces no good results. It breaks down moral restraints and causes a person to say things he would never say otherwise. A person who drinks often places himself in danger of immediate death due to the effects of intoxication, not to mention the long-term, addictive results of alcohol.

Isaiah 5:11
> *Woe unto them that rise up early in the morning, that they may follow strong drink; that continue until night, till wine inflame them!*

Isaiah 28:7
> *But they also have erred through wine, and through strong drink are out of the way; the priest and the prophet have erred through strong drink, they are swallowed up of wine, they are out of the way through strong drink; they err in vision, they stumble in judgment.*

These verses show the addictive nature of intoxicating beverages and the fact that those who partake of them will err in matters of judgment. The reason for this is their senses are polluted.

It is the third category of references that prompts some to excuse alcoholic beverages, often with the hopeful intention to drink in moderation. There is no way to know how many have fallen into the treacherous trap of drunkenness by prefacing their imbibing with, "After all, didn't Paul tell Timothy to take a little wine for his stomach's sake?"

It is important to understand there are two kinds of wines mentioned in Scripture. As William Patton said in *Bible Wines or Laws of Fermentation And Wines of the Ancient*, "There were ...

two kinds of wine in ancient use. The one was sweet, pleasant, refreshing, unfermented; the other was exciting, inflaming, intoxicating. Each was called wine."[30]

Patton meticulously documented the fact that unfermented beverages, called wines, existed and were commonly used by the ancients. He gives abundant proof of the generic nature of the two Hebrew words, *yayin* and *shakar*.[31]

Yayin (translated in the KJV as "wine") "designates grape juice, or the liquid which the fruit of the vine yields. This may be new or old, sweet or sour, fermented or unfermented, intoxicating or unintoxicating."[32]

Shakar (translated as "strong drink") "'signifies "sweet drink" expressed from fruits other than the grape, and drunk in an unfermented or fermented state.'"[33]

These two words are generic. The Scripture uses them to refer to both fermented and unfermented drinks. The context determines which meaning is intended.

There are other relevant Hebrew words that always carry the same meaning. One of the most common is *tirosh* (translated as "wine," "new wine," and "sweet wine"). This "wine" is an unfermented drink. The term generally refers to the juice of something other than the grape; for example, corn and olives.

The New Testament uses a generic Greek word, *oinos,* to correspond exactly to *yayin* in the Old Testament. It, too, designates the juice of the grape in all its stages. The context must determine whether fermented or unfermented beverage is meant.

The English word "wine" is from the Latin *vinum* (or *vinus*), which is equivalent to the Greek *oinos*. The Latin word is generic, referring to the juice of the grape in all its forms. This concept was brought into the English word *wine*. During the era when the KJV

---

[30] Patton, William, *The Laws of Fermentation and the Wines of the Ancients*, National Temperance Society and Publication House, 1872.

[31] *Ibid.*

[32] *Ibid.*

[33] *Ibid.*

was translated, that meaning was universally accepted. More recent dictionaries will define *wine* exclusively as a fermented beverage, but we must be careful not to allow modern-day usage of a word to be retroactively applied to a 400-year-old translation.

The reason for the development of the restricted meaning of wine to fermented liquid only is described by John Stuart Mill in his *System of Logic:* "A generic term is always liable to become limited to a single species if people have occasion to think and speak of that species oftener than of anything else contained in the genus. The tide of custom first drifts the word on the shore of a particular meaning, then retires and leaves it there."[34] In other words, he stated that it is common for some generic term to eventually be used exclusively with a specific meaning rather than in the more expansive concept originally intended. Such is the case for the word "wine." Although it once referred to ANY liquid pressed from grapes, it has become more limited in modern times.

What, then, did Paul mean when he said to Timothy, "Drink no longer water, but use a little wine for thy stomach's sake and thine often infirmities" (I Timothy 5:23)? Did he command Timothy to indulge in fermented alcoholic beverages for the sake of a weak stomach? Such would seem to be precisely the wrong prescription if fermented wine was intended. Indeed, the fermented wines of that day produced "headaches, dropsy, madness, and stomach complaints."[35] At the same time, there were unfermented wines that were "exceedingly wholesome and useful to the body."[36]

Paul, who had earlier told Timothy that a bishop must not be given to wine (I Timothy 3:3), knew the inherent evil of fermented wine from the law ("wine is a mocker"). He would not have recommended to Timothy such a forbidden, dangerous substance to drink in place of water.

Some make their plea for moderate use of alcohol based on a

---

[34] Mill, John Stuart, *System of Logic,* Baptist Missionary Press, 1821.

[35] Patton, William, *The Laws of Fermentation and the Wines of the Ancients,* National Temperance Society and Publication House, New York, 1872.

[36] *Ibid.*

misunderstanding of Ephesians 5:18: "And be not drunk with wine, wherein is excess ... ." They point out that one is not to drink to excess, or until he is drunk.

The literal meaning of the Greek word translated *excess* is, however, "dissolution, dissipation." In this case, the word *excess* does not refer to quantity but to that which is inherent in fermented wine. The phrase "wherein is" reveals the "excess" is *in the wine*. In other words, the use of fermented wine dissipates.

The word "dissipate" is defined as: "1. To drive away; cause to vanish; 2. To spend or expend intemperately or wastefully; squander. 3. To use up, especially recklessly; exhaust; 4. To cause to lose (energy, such as heat) irreversibly."[37]

According to Dr. Amanda N. McDonald, "There is no designated 'safe' level of drinking."[38] Another professional wrote, "As soon as someone takes a sip of alcohol, it starts to enter their bloodstream."[39] One could say that the first drink of alcohol intoxicates. After that, the drunkenness is only a matter of degree.

Consider the following statistics:

- "About 178,000 people die from excessive drinking each year. These deaths occur from both drinking alcohol over several years or drinking too much on one occasion."[40]

- "Every day, about 37 people in the United States die in drunk-driving crashes — that's one person every 39 minutes. In 2022, 13,524 people died in alcohol-impaired driving traffic deaths. These deaths were all preventable."[41]

---

[37] Wordnik.com, https://www.wordnik.com/words/dissipate

[38] Northwestern Medicine, https://www.nm.org/healthbeat/healthy-tips/alcohol-and-the-brain, Updated November, 2023.

[39] Richards, Louisa, and Cynthia Taylor Chavoustie, MPAS, PA-C, Medical News Today, https://www.medicalnewstoday.com/articles/how-many-drinks-does-it-take-to-get-drunk, Updated September 26, 2023.

[40] Centers for Disease Control, *Facts About U.S. Deaths from Excessive Alcohol Use*, https://www.cdc.gov/alcohol/facts-stats/index.html

[41] National Highway Safety Administration, *Drunk Driving*, https://www.nhtsa.gov/risky-driving/drunk-driving

o About 90 percent of unwanted pregnancies result from alcohol-lowered inhibitions. About 36 percent of suicide victims have a history of alcohol abuse or were drinking shortly before taking their own lives.[42]

The person who refuses to drink will never have to worry about drinking too much. He will never be guilty of drunkenness but will live a life free from the ravages of liquor.

- **Smoking**

It is a highly documented fact that smoking contributes to cancer of the lungs, mouth, and lips. So convincing is the evidence that the United States Surgeon General won the fight to have a warning placed on every package of cigarettes and every advertisement for cigarettes. This happened in 1965!

Make no mistake: tobacco is a habit-forming narcotic. Among unbiased researchers, there is no question as to the devastating effect of smoking on the human body.

Many godly men took a firm stand against the use of tobacco years before medical research determined its danger. How did they have the foresight to avoid this dangerous practice? The Spirit obviously directed them to make this stand. Still, they no doubt wanted some Biblical principle they could use to verify the sinfulness of this practice.

While there is no verse that says, "Thou shalt not smoke," there are many verses of Scripture instructing us to avoid coming under the power of any substance. A Christian should even resist falling under the power of which things might be considered "lawful practices."

> ***1 Corinthians 6:12***
> *All things are lawful unto me, but all things are not expedient: all things are lawful for me, but I will not be brought under the power of any.*

---

[42] Mitchell, Ben, *The Works of the Flesh (Galatians 5:19)*, published by the Christian Life Commission of the Southern Baptist Convention, Nashville, TN [date unknown].

Understanding Separation

I will deal with this verse in more detail momentarily, but suffice it to say it very plainly prohibits any child of God from becoming addicted to any substance. God does not want anything to dictate our lives other than Him. The American Cancer Society states, "Studies have found that nicotine addiction can be just as strong as addiction to substances like cocaine and alcohol. In fact, tobacco may be even harder for some people to quit."[43]

As the first verse addressed in this chapter points out, God will judge anyone who defiles the temple of God (see 1 Corinthians 3:16-17). There is no question that tobacco defiles the body, which is His temple. Tobacco usage coats the lungs with tar, promotes various ailments, including cancer, and robs the smoker of vitality, alertness, and years of life.

It has been reported that "more than 16 million Americans are living with a disease caused by smoking. Across the world, tobacco causes more than 7 million deaths per year. On average, smokers die 10 years earlier than nonsmokers."[44]

Would God have approved of a vandal entering His Holy of Holies in the Tabernacle and painting the Ark of the Covenant with a tar brush? Of course He wouldn't! Neither would He approve of His child defiling the temple of our body.

Consider further the effects of secondhand smoke. "Inhaling other people's smoke causes you to breathe in these toxins. Smoke from the end of a burning cigarette, cigar or pipe is unfiltered. It may have even more harmful toxins than tobacco smoke that someone breathes out. There are over 7,000 chemicals in tobacco smoke. About 69 of these chemicals are known to cause cancer (carcinogens). About 250 of the chemicals are known to be harmful to your health."[45] Thus, those who smoke are not only

---

[43] American Cancer Society, *Why People Start Smoking and Why its Hard to Stop*, https://www.cancer.org/cancer/risk-prevention/tobacco/guide-quitting-smoking/why-people-start-using-tobacco.html

[44] Johns Hopkins Medicine, *5 Vaping Facts You Need to Know*, https://www.hopkinsmedicine.org/health/wellness-and-prevention/5-truths-you-need-to-know-about-vaping

[45] Cleveland Clinic, *Second Hand Smoke,*

damaging their OWN body-temples, but they are causing perhaps even MORE damage to the temples of others!

Secondhand smoke "causes more than 7,000 lung cancer deaths each year in people who don't smoke. And it causes a total of 41,000 other deaths per year. It can also lead to lung conditions and heart disease."[46]

In 1 Corinthians 6, Paul makes a fascinating statement. Please pay attention to how he connects what is done in the body to what happens in our spirit.

1 Corinthians 6:15-17

Know ye not that your bodies are the members of Christ? shall I then take the members of Christ, and make them the members of an harlot? God forbid. [16]What? know ye not that he which is joined to an harlot is one body? for two, saith he, shall be one flesh. [17]But he that is joined unto the Lord is one spirit.

The Apostle argues that our fleshly actions have direct spiritual ramifications. The ungodly practices in which a Christian engages actually affect the entire body of Christ. I contend that just as fornication "joins the members of Christ" to the object of that sin, so the use of tobacco "joins" His members to the vile contents being delivered to the user. Such individuals not only defile themselves but, by extension, they defile their brothers and sisters in the Lord!

Such defilement, by the way, occurs regardless of the method of delivery. Whether cigars, cigarettes, chewing tobacco, or vaping, introducing carcinogens, addictive chemicals, and other unhealthy ingredients will bring damage to our health. God will surely judge those who defile His temple.

With regard to vaping, it should be noted that "The liquid

---

https://my.clevelandclinic.org/health/articles/10644-secondhand-smoke-dangers

[46] Johns Hopkins Medicine, *Smoking and Respiratory Diseases*, https://www.hopkinsmedicine.org/health/conditions-and-diseases/smoking-and-respiratory-diseases

used in e-cigarettes usually contains harmful substances such as nicotine, heavy metals, and known carcinogens such as formaldehyde that can have negative effects on lung health, cardiovascular health, and overall well-being."[47] The way an e-cigarette (or "vape") works is that it will "heat a liquid and produce an aerosol."[48] The person vaping then "inhales this aerosol into their lungs. Bystanders can also breathe in the aerosol when the person using the e-cigarette breathes the aerosol out."[49]

"In February 2020, the Centers for Disease Control and Prevention (CDC) confirmed 2,807 cases of e-cigarette or vaping use-associated lung injury (EVALI) and 68 deaths attributed to that condition. Both e-cigarettes and regular cigarettes contain nicotine, which research suggests may be as addictive as heroin and cocaine [and] what's worse [is that] many e-cigarette users get even more nicotine than they would from a combustible tobacco product."[50]

Obviously, then, everything that has been said about the use of tobacco applies to vaping as well. It, too, defiles God's holy temple – both for the participant and for those around him.

- **Drugs**

In many ways, all that has previously been said about alcohol and tobacco applies equally to the abuse of drugs. Unlike alcohol and tobacco, there is a scripturally endorsed use for medicine.

Proverbs 17:22

A merry heart doeth good like a medicine: but a broken spirit drieth the bones.

Note the phrase "good like a medicine." If all medicine were

---

[47] American Heart Association, *What You Need to Know about Vaping*, https://www.heart.org/en/health-topics/house-calls/what-you-need-to-know-about-vaping

[48] Centers for Disease Control, *Smoking and Tobacco Use*, https://www.cdc.gov/tobacco/e-cigarettes/about.html

[49] *Ibid.*

[50] Johns Hopkins Medicine, *5 Vaping Facts You Need to Know*, https://www.hopkinsmedicine.org/health/wellness-and-prevention/5-truths-you-need-to-know-about-vaping

evil, this phrase would not be found in the Scriptures!

Jeremiah 8:22

Is there no balm in Gilead; is there no physician there? why then is not the health of the daughter of my people recovered?

When the prophet spoke of "balm" and "physicians," he certainly did not prohibit their use. Instead, he implies that it is not only acceptable to use doctors and medicine, it is expected.

Revelation 3:18

I counsel thee to buy of me gold tried in the fire, that thou mayest be rich; and white raiment, that thou mayest be clothed, and that the shame of thy nakedness do not appear; and anoint thine eyes with eyesalve, that thou mayest see.

Although He was speaking in a spiritual sense, Jesus still spoke of the value of using "eyesalve" when needed. The Lord would not have used this analogy if medication had been a sin. In Matthew's gospel, He actually spoke of the benefits physicians provide to the sick.

Matthew 9:12

But when Jesus heard that, he said unto them, They that be whole need not a physician, but they that are sick.

Luke was referred to as a physician long after his conversion. One example is found in Paul's letter to the church at Colosse.

Colossians 4:14

Luke, the beloved physician, and Demas, greet you.

Despite all this, one should not trust solely in physicians or medicines. Instead, one's trust must be in the Lord, and He must be recognized as the source of all healing. Many question the wisdom of the modern medical profession concerning drugs. Ethical problems occur, specifically with the frequent prescription of placebos. One national news source reported that "more than half of doctors offer fake prescriptions."[51]

Aside from the questions of drug use as related to the medical profession, we are currently facing an epidemic of drug abuse by people of all ages. The problem ranges from those who smoke marijuana to Valium addicts.

As has already been pointed out, a Christian must not allow himself to come under the power of anything that is habit-forming. This, of course, includes drugs.

1 Corinthians 6:12
All things are lawful unto me, but all things are not expedient: all things are lawful for me, but I will not be brought under the power of any.

The word "power," as it is used here, means "control." The apostle was simply saying we should not allow ourselves to be under the control of any substance. Perhaps the greatest gift God gave to humanity as a whole (outside of salvation, of course) is a conscience. He also granted us a free will. Both of these are negatively impacted – and often become obscured – when we become addicted to something.

It has been documented repeatedly in volumes of scientific and medical reports that drug abuse is a deadly pursuit. The only individuals who question these findings are those who, for personal gain or pleasure, wish to excuse the abuse of drugs. They might insist that some grand, mysterious conspiracy exists to keep them from experiencing the harmless pleasures of drugs.

If that is true, where are the healthy drug addicts? There are none! As has been witnessed repeatedly, drugs mercilessly kill those who have done the most to popularize their use.

The Greek word that is translated as "witchcraft" or "sorcery" in our English New Testament is *pharmakeia*, the same word from which we get "pharmacy." It implies the abuse of drugs to induce altered states of consciousness to aid in occultic

---

[51] CBS News, *50% of Doctors Prescribe Placebos*, https://www.cbsnews.com/news/50-of-doctors-prescribe-placebos

practices.

This is listed with the works of the flesh in Galatians 5:20. It is one of the things that will keep us from the kingdom of God.

What effect does drug abuse have on our society? "A study at 7 trauma centers of 4,243 drivers who were seriously injured in crashes found that 54% of drivers tested positive for alcohol and/or drugs from September 2019 to July 2021. Of the 4,243 drivers, 22% were positive for alcohol, 25% were positive for marijuana, 9% were positive for opioids, 10% were positive for stimulants, and 8% were positive for sedatives."[52]

Death is not the only tragic outcome of drugs. "Studies suggest that a parent with a substance use disorder is 3 times more likely to physically or sexually abuse their child."[53]

There is no justification for the use of illegal drugs by Christians. It is a mind-altering, violence-producing, habit-forming, disease-developing practice which must be shunned as yet another satanic attempt to defile the temple of God.

- **Gluttony**

I realize this may hit close to home for many. Nevertheless, it IS a Scriptural topic and should be addressed as such.

Let me begin by saying, however, that not EVERYONE who is overweight is a glutton. Genetics, medical conditions, poor food choices, and other factors can cause obesity. I have no room to criticize anyone for carrying extra pounds inasmuch as I have struggled with my weight for decades. In fact, if the current weight charts are the guide, I am considerably overweight.

The word "gluttony" means "the over-indulgence or lack of self-restraint in food, drink, or wealth items, especially as status tokens. The English word comes from the Latin and means 'to

---

[52] Centers for Disease Control, *Impaired Driving*, https://www.cdc.gov/impaired-driving/facts/index.html

[53] American Addiction Centers, *The Link Between Child Abuse and Substance Abuse*, https://americanaddictioncenters.org/blog/the-link-between-child-abuse-and-substance-abuse

gulp.' Gluttony worships food to feed our own self-love."[54]

"Gluttony seems to be a sin that Christians like to ignore. We are often quick to label smoking and drinking as sins, but for some reason, gluttony is accepted or at least tolerated. Many of the arguments used against smoking and drinking, such as health and addiction, apply equally to overeating. Many ... would not even consider having a glass of wine or smoking a cigarette, but have no qualms about gorging themselves ... to the point that they feel like they are going to explode. This should not be!"[55]

The Bible has much to say on this subject. The problem is none of it is positive.

Proverbs 23:20-21

Be not among winebibbers; among riotous eaters of flesh: 21For the drunkard and the glutton shall come to poverty: and drowsiness shall clothe a man with rags.

Proverbs 28:7

Whoso keepeth the law is a wise son: but he that is a companion of riotous men shameth his father.

Many other translations render "riotous men" as "gluttons." That is one of the ways the original Hebrew word can rightfully be translated. If that is the proper interpretation, Solomon felt that even associating with gluttonous people is a shameful practice.

Job 15:27

Because he covereth his face with his fatness, and maketh collops of fat on his flanks.

The word "collops" literally means "pieces of flesh." One

---

[54] Christianity.com, *What is the Sin of Gluttony, and What are its Consequences?*, https://www.christianity.com/wiki/sin/what-is-the-sin-of-gluttony-its-definition-and-consequences.html

[55] Paulose, Dr. K.O., *Gluttony – Is it a Sin?*, https://drpaulose.com/spirituality/gluttony-is-it-a-sin

well-known commentary renders it "masses of fat."[56]

The *World English Bible* says, "Because he has covered his face with his fatness, and gathered fat on his thighs."[57] *The New King James* reads, "Though he has covered his face with his fatness, and made his waist heavy with fat."[58] *The Holman Christian Standard Bible* translates this as "his face is covered with fat and his waistline bulges with it."[59] *The 1899 Douay-Rheims Bible* renders it, "Fatness hath covered his face, and the fat hangeth down on his sides."[60]

When referring to this "fatness," of whom was Eliphaz speaking? One only needs to back up a few verses to find the answer. Verse 20 identifies the subject as "the wicked man."

It appears that, at least in Job's day, "fatness" was a sign of "wickedness." This idea is not limited to that time period, however. Consider how God described the rebellion of Israel.

> ***Deuteronomy 32:15***
> *But Jeshurun waxed fat, and kicked: thou art waxen fat, thou art grown thick, thou art covered with fatness; then he forsook God which made him, and lightly esteemed the Rock of his salvation.*

The Christian Standard Bible reads, "Then Jeshurun became fat and rebelled—you became fat, bloated, and gorged. He abandoned the God who made him and scorned the Rock of his salvation."[61] *The Message Bible* says, "Jeshurun put on weight and bucked; you got fat, became obese, a tub of lard. He abandoned

---

[56] Jamieson, Robert, Andrew Robert Fausset, and David Brown, *Commentary on the Whole Bible*. Originally published 1871.

[57] *World English Bible*, Librivox, 2017.

[58] *The New King James Bible*, Worldwide Publishers, 2017.

[59] *Holman Christian Standard Bible*, Holman Bible Publishers, 2004.

[60] *Douay-Rheims Bible*, Loreto Publications, 2020.

[61] *Holman Christian Standard Bible*, Holman Bible Publishers, 2004.

the God who made him, he mocked the Rock of his salvation."[62]

While I understand (and have experienced) the struggle of maintaining a healthy weight, I do think we can be guilty of hypocrisy if we are willing to "defile the temple of our bodies" through uncontrolled eating while decrying those who defile it in other ways. We must bring our bodies under subjection, just as the Apostle Paul did.

1 Corinthians 9:27
> But I keep under my body, and bring it into subjection: lest that by any means, when I have preached to others, I myself should be a castaway.

The *Contemporary English Version* offers insight into precisely what Paul meant. It reads, "I keep my body under control and make it my slave, so I won't lose out after telling the good news to others."[63]

- **Body Modifications**

Please understand that I am NOT talking specifically about "sex change" (or "gender reassignment") surgeries – although that could definitely be included, and everything I am about to say most assuredly applies. What I am talking about is making ANY modifications to your body through things like piercings, tattoos, "cuttings," and other forms of what can rightfully be considered "mutilation" of your body as God created it.

The word "mutilate" means "disfiguring" or in any way bringing injury or change to your body with the intent of having a permanent effect. Before looking at the specific Scriptural prohibitions, we should first ask ourselves a few questions about the MOTIVE behind having some kind of "piercing," tattoo, or such like.

Proverbs 16:2
> All the ways of a man are clean in his own eyes;

---

[62] Peterson, Eugene, *The Message Bible,* Playaway Publishers, 2010.

[63] *The Contemporary English Version,* Thomas Nelson Publishers, 1995.

but the LORD weigheth the spirits.

The *Common English Version* says, "We may think we know what is right, but the LORD is the judge of our motives."[64] Our motives matter; we should never do something just to be like the world.

To help determine our motive, here are some specific questions we need to answer:

(1) Am I trying to identify with a particular culture OTHER than the church?

2 Corinthians 6:17-18

Wherefore come out from among them, and be ye separate, saith the Lord, and touch not the unclean thing; and I will receive you, [18]And will be a Father unto you, and ye shall be my sons and daughters, saith the Lord Almighty.

(2) Am I yielding to peer pressure?

Galatians 1:10

For do I now persuade men, or God? or do I seek to please men? for if I yet pleased men, I should not be the servant of Christ.

(3) Am I more concerned about my outer appearance than I am about my inner man?

2 Corinthians 10:7

Do ye look on things after the outward appearance? If any man trust to himself that he is Christ's, let him of himself think this again, that, as he is Christ's, even so are we Christ's.

(4) Am I drawing undue attention to my flesh?

1 Peter 5:5

Likewise, ye younger, submit yourselves unto

---

[64] *The Contemporary English Version*, Thomas Nelson Publishers, 1995.

> the elder. Yea, all of you be subject one to another, and be clothed with humility: for God resisteth the proud, and giveth grace to the humble.

The Bible in Basic English translates this verse by saying, "Let all of you put away pride and make yourselves ready to be servants: for God is a hater of pride, but he gives grace to those who make themselves low."[65]

After answering all of these questions, you should recognize that there are problems with piercings, tattoos, and other "body modifications." If not, consider what the Bible has to say directly on this subject.

Deuteronomy 15:17
> Then thou shalt take an aul, and thrust it through his ear unto the door, and he shall be thy servant for ever. And also unto thy maidservant thou shalt do likewise.

God instituted piercing the ear as a sign of perpetual slavery. It was a mark to the world that a person had chosen to give up the freedom they had been offered.

Leviticus 19:28
> Ye shall not make any cuttings in your flesh for the dead, nor print any marks upon you: I am the LORD.

God's Word Translation closes this verse by saying, "Never get a tattoo. I am the LORD."[66] How much clearer can it be said?

Don't misunderstand this verse by thinking it is ONLY against "cuttings ... for the dead." Although that's the main thrust, there is an overarching principle. It is clear from Scripture that "cutting" (or "piercing," for that matter) is associated with idolatry and demonic activity.

---

[65] Hooke, S. H., *The Bible in Basic English*, Cambridge University Press, 1982.
[66] *God's Word Translation*, Baker Books, 2010.

1 Kings 18:25-28

And Elijah said unto the prophets of Baal, Choose you one bullock for yourselves, and dress it first; for ye are many; and call on the name of your gods, but put no fire under. ²⁶And they took the bullock which was given them, and they dressed it, and called on the name of Baal from morning even until noon, saying, O Baal, hear us. But there was no voice, nor any that answered. And they leaped upon the altar which was made. ²⁷And it came to pass at noon, that Elijah mocked them, and said, Cry aloud: for he is a god; either he is talking, or he is pursuing, or he is in a journey, or peradventure he sleepeth, and must be awaked. ²⁸And they cried aloud, and cut themselves after their manner with knives and lancets, till the blood gushed out upon them.

Once again, let us consider the verses we dealt with when we opened this chapter. Although I try not to be redundant, it is worth looking at again.

1 Corinthians 3:16-17

Know ye not that ye are the temple of God, and that the Spirit of God dwelleth in you? ¹⁷If any man defile the temple of God, him shall God destroy; for the temple of God is holy, which temple ye are.

According to *Thayer's*, "In the opinion of the Jews, the temple was corrupted or 'destroyed' when anyone defiled or **in the slightest degree damaged anything in it**, or if its guardians neglected their duties."[67] *[Emphasis added.]* Piercings, tattoos, and other methods of making modifications to our bodies would undoubtedly fit into this definition.

---

[67] Thayer, J., *A Greek-English Lexicon of the New Testament,* Baker Book House, 1993.

- **"Such Like"**

Things we've discussed so far are not the only ways in which a Christian can defile the holy temple of his body. There are many others, including fornication and other forms of immorality (which I deal with in chapter 10 of this book). Nevertheless, these are a few of the most common and visible ways. They must be shunned at all costs. The Christian who makes these stands will shine as a bright light in a dark, corrupt world.

In conclusion, we must remember that we are not our own, for we have been bought with a price (see 1 Corinthians 6:19-20). Therefore, we have an obligation to God to live our lives in accordance with the dictates of His Holy Word. Paul called it our "reasonable service."

Romans 12:1

I beseech you therefore, brethren, by the mercies of God, that ye present your bodies a living sacrifice, holy, acceptable unto God, which is your reasonable service.

Present Your Bodies

GUARDING YOUR TONGUE

Psalm 141:3
Set a watch, O LORD, before my mouth; keep the door of my lips.

According to the Apostle James, there is one thing that is virtually impossible for humanity to accomplish. That one thing is taming the tongue.

James 3:7-8
For every kind of beasts, and of birds, and of serpents, and of things in the sea, is tamed, and hath been tamed of mankind: ⁸But the tongue can no man tame; it is an unruly evil, full of deadly poison.

In my opinion, this is one reason God chose speaking in tongues as the evidence that someone has been filled with the Holy Ghost. In causing us to speak words we don't understand, He is showing the world He can control the one thing we cannot.

Sadly, it is far too easy for us to "speak our mind" without giving it much thought. However, we need to recognize the extent of power inherent in our words.

Proverbs 18:21
Death and life are in the power of the tongue: and they that love it shall eat the fruit thereof.

Guarding Your Tongue

As a child, I was taught to tell those who said hurtful things to me, "Sticks and stones may break my bones, but words can never hurt me."[68] It sounds good, but unfortunately, it is simply not true. The wounds caused by "sticks and stones" will generally heal over time. On the other hand, the damage done by spiteful conversation can last a lifetime.

Not only can the things we say hurt others, but we can do spiritual damage to ourselves because of what comes out of our mouths. The Lord stated that justification and condemnation are brought about by our words.

> **Matthew 12:37**
> *For by thy words thou shalt be justified, and by thy words thou shalt be condemned.*

King Solomon had much to say about the power of our words. Among other things, he said they can bring either healing or destruction.

> **Proverbs 6:2**
> *Thou art snared with the words of thy mouth, thou art taken with the words of thy mouth.*

> **Proverbs 12:18**
> *There is that speaketh like the piercings of a sword: but the tongue of the wise is health.*

> **Proverbs 13:3**
> *He that keepeth his mouth keepeth his life: but he that openeth wide his lips shall have destruction.*

> **Proverbs 15:4**
> *A wholesome tongue is a tree of life: but*

---

[68] The author of this rhyme is unknown. However, it evidently appeared in print as an unattributed quote as far back as the mid-1800's.

perverseness therein is a breach in the spirit.

Some people are able to speak things that bring emotional healing like a soothing balm. The words of others are like a sword. Included in his instructions to the church at Thessalonica, Paul gave a specific command concerning what we say. He told them to "study to be quiet."

1 Thessalonians 4:11
And that ye study to be quiet, and to do your own business, and to work with your own hands, as we commanded you;

Barnes' Notes on the New Testament explains the literal meaning of the Greek: "Make it your ambition to be quiet, and to do your own business." He goes on to say this is "in direct contrast to the world's ambition, which is, 'to make a great stir,' and 'to be busybodies.'"[69]

Abraham Lincoln supposedly said it is better to remain silent and be thought a fool than to open your mouth and remove all doubt.[70] The principle behind this concept is Biblical.

Proverbs 17:28
Even a fool, when he holdeth his peace, is counted wise: and he that shutteth his lips is esteemed a man of understanding.

A woman once told John Wesley, "My talent is to speak my mind." Wesley reportedly responded, "I am sure, Sister, that God would not object if you buried that talent."[71]

---

[69] Barnes, A., J. G. Murphy, F. C. Cook, E. B. Pusey, H.C. Leupold, & R. Frew, *Barnes' Notes*. Blackie & Son, 1847.

[70] *Golden Book Magazine*, Volume 14, Published by The Review of Reviews Corporation, 1931.

[71] Guzik, David. Study Guide for James 3, *Warnings and Words to Teachers*, Blue Letter Bible, 2018, https://www.blueletterbible.org/comm/guzik_david/study-guide/james/james-3.cfm

As Apostolics, we undoubtedly have many ideas as to what "spirituality" looks like. Perhaps it's based on the frequency or intensity of one's worship. It might be based on other things like following the guidelines of the local assembly. These are great qualities. However, the New Testament provides us with a "sure-fire" test that, while it may not show how spiritual we ARE, definitely shows how spiritual we are NOT!

> **James 1:26**
> *If any man among you seem to be religious, and bridleth not his tongue, but deceiveth his own heart, this man's religion is vain.*

As I have already stated, it matters little if (for example) a woman has long hair and wears long skirts and long sleeves, if she also has a long tongue. James says in unequivocal terms that anyone who does not "bridle" his tongue is practicing vain religion. *The Contemporary English Version* says, "If you think you are being religious but can't control your tongue, you are fooling yourself, and everything you do is useless."[72]

The importance of guarding our mouths cannot be overemphasized. Jesus said we must give an account for EVERY idle word.

> **Matthew 12:36**
> *But I say unto you, That every idle word that men shall speak, they shall give account thereof in the day of judgment.*

Vine's Expository Dictionary says the word "idle" means "barren, yielding no return."[73] The author goes on to say that in this particular verse, it means "the word that is thoughtless or

---

[72] *The Contemporary English Version*, Thomas Nelson Publishers, 1995.

[73] Vine, W.E., J.R. Kohlenberger, J.A. Swanson, *The Expanded Vine's Expository Dictionary of New Testament Words.* Bethany House Publishers, 1984.

profitless."[74] God is keeping a record of the things we utter. We should strive to keep that record as guiltless as possible.

The first chapter of the Book of James states that a lack of verbal carefulness is the result of "vain religion." In the third chapter, the apostle shows us the opposite is also true. Being able to hold our tongue is a sign of spiritual maturity.

James 3:2
For in many things we offend all. If any man offend not in word, the same is a perfect man, and able also to bridle the whole body.

Christians who know how to discipline their words are of great blessing and value to the church. Their ability to hold their peace when necessary, yet say the appropriate words when the occasion requires, is very edifying.

Proverbs 25:11
A word fitly spoken is like apples of gold in pictures of silver.

We should diligently try to use our words for positive and constructive purposes. Perhaps Paul had this in mind when he instructed Titus to maintain "sound speech."

Titus 2:8
Sound speech, that cannot be condemned; that he that is of the contrary part may be ashamed, having no evil thing to say of you.

The Greek word translated "sound" simply means "healthy" or, by implication, "true." *Thayer's Greek Lexicon* says the connotation is something "wholesome, fit, [or] wise."[75] These are

---

[74] Vine, W.E., J.R. Kohlenberger, J.A. Swanson, *The Expanded Vine's Expository Dictionary of New Testament Words.* Bethany House Publishers, 1984.

[75] Thayer, J., *A Greek-English Lexicon of the New Testament,* Baker Book House, 1993.

the kind of words that ought to come naturally to the child of God.

The Psalmist David evidently understood well the absolute need for us to guard our tongues. He prayed for God to place a guard in front of his mouth.

Psalm 141:3
Set a watch, O LORD, before my mouth; keep the door of my lips.

Such a prayer should be ours as well. We need the Master's help and guidance to keep us from speaking things we ought not.

Let us take some time now to examine four specific areas over which we must gain control. Each of these could easily be addressed in a book all its own.

- **Lying**

In describing those who would suffer eternal judgment, Jesus listed some vile sins. Notice, however, the last group He mentioned.

Revelation 21:8
But the fearful, and unbelieving, and the abominable, and murderers, and whoremongers, and sorcerers, and idolaters, and all liars, shall have their part in the lake which burneth with fire and brimstone: which is the second death.

Interestingly, He only added the word "all" when He spoke of liars. It appears He wanted to ensure everyone understood that even something people might categorize as a "white" lie still qualifies as a lie!

He spoke so strongly about lying because it is not just a sin. It is an abomination!

Proverbs 6:16-19
These six things doth the LORD hate: yea, seven are an abomination unto him: [17]A proud look, a

lying tongue, and hands that shed innocent blood, ¹⁸An heart that deviseth wicked imaginations, feet that be swift in running to mischief, ¹⁹A false witness that speaketh lies, and he that soweth discord among brethren.

The subject of abominations will be addressed more fully in another chapter. For now, just know the word indicates something terribly loathsome and detestable.

While some religions claim the "seven deadly sins" are "pride, greed, wrath, envy, lust, gluttony, and sloth," The list in this passage in Proverbs says something different. Here, when relating the seven things God REALLY hates, he includes a form of lying as TWO of the seven!

Lying is in direct contradiction to God's very nature. He doesn't just speak truth. He IS Truth! (See John 14:6.)

Lies originate from Satan himself. Jesus said the devil is the "father" of lies (see John 8:44).

One form of lying which seems to be acceptable to some people is flattery. Regardless, it is certainly not acceptable to God.

Psalm 78:36

Nevertheless they did flatter him with their mouth, and they lied unto him with their tongues.

I once read about a man who had a unique way of explaining the problem of flattery. He began by asking, "If you call the tail of a dog 'a leg,' how many legs would a dog have?" When the answer rang out, "Five," he replied, "You're wrong! It would still have only FOUR. Calling a tail a leg does not make it one!"

Just because someone says you are "great" or "wise" (or whatever) does not make it so. We shouldn't swallow their attempts at flattery! Nor should we attempt to flatter others because the Scripture states flattery is a characteristic of wickedness.

Psalm 5:9

For there is no faithfulness in their mouth; their inward part is very wickedness; their throat is an open sepulchre; they flatter with their tongue.

Psalm 12:2

They speak vanity every one with his neighbour: with flattering lips and with a double heart do they speak.

Flattery is a characteristic of deception. God's Word warns us emphatically that this is the case.

Proverbs 29:5

A man that flattereth his neighbour spreadeth a net for his feet.

Becoming susceptible to flattery is extremely dangerous on many fronts. This is especially true in the case of harlotry.

Proverbs 2:16

To deliver thee from the strange woman, even from the stranger which flattereth with her words;

Proverbs 6:24

To keep thee from the evil woman, from the flattery of the tongue of a strange woman.

Proverbs 7:5

That they may keep thee from the strange woman, from the stranger which flattereth with her words.

Proverbs 7:21

With her much fair speech she caused him to yield, with the flattering of her lips she forced him.

The Bible tells us how to treat those who practice flattery. We are instructed to avoid them.

Proverbs 20:19
He that goeth about as a talebearer revealeth secrets: therefore meddle not with him that flattereth with his lips.

Those who practice flattery will be judged. Scripture makes that abundantly clear.

Job 17:5
He that speaketh flattery to his friends, even the eyes of his children shall fail.

Psalm 12:3
The LORD shall cut off all flattering lips, and the tongue that speaketh proud things:

Proverbs 26:28
A lying tongue hateth those that are afflicted by it; and a flattering mouth worketh ruin.

- **Profanity**

Leviticus 19:12
And ye shall not swear by my name falsely, neither shalt thou profane the name of thy God: I am the LORD.

There was a time when people were extremely conscientious – and careful – about how and when they spoke the Lord's name. It seems, however, that something has happened which has caused many to be much more relaxed about it. Nevertheless, the Bible has not changed its prohibition against this practice.

Exodus 20:7
Thou shalt not take the name of the LORD thy God in vain; for the LORD will not hold him guiltless that taketh his name in vain.

> ***Deuteronomy 5:11***
> *Thou shalt not take the name of the* LORD *thy God in vain: for the* LORD *will not hold him guiltless that taketh his name in vain.*

The phrase "in vain" means "without purpose." We should be much more careful about using "Lord," "Jesus," or "God." If we are not speaking TO Him or ABOUT Him, there is a good chance we are using His name as nothing more than a byword. Far too often, Christians carelessly exclaim (and/or type), "OMG." Those letters represent the use of a term which for many years was considered profaning God's name. (Hint: the "G" does NOT stand for "goodness," although the One Who IS being referenced IS good.)

Many saints would never consider speaking a cuss word. However, we must also beware of "slang" – words that mean the same thing but sound less offensive.

> ***Romans 14:16***
> *Let not then your good be evil spoken of:*

I do not personally feel comfortable even typing out some of the terms I have heard Apostolics toss around freely. Instead, I will simply suggest that every reader consider whether the words and phrases they use are "acceptable in God's sight." (See Psalm 19:14.)

- **Gossip**

> ***Leviticus 19:16***
> *Thou shalt not go up and down as a talebearer among thy people: neither shalt thou stand against the blood of thy neighbour: I am the* LORD.

In my more than 50 years of serving God, it has been my experience that few things have done as much damage to the work of God as gossip has. The devastation caused by spreading rumors has been far-reaching. It would never even be a consideration if we truly love our neighbor as ourselves.

The following phrases are very likely an opening for gossip. "Don't say I told you, but..." or "Can you imagine...?" or "Everyone is saying..." are red flags that a conversation is about to ensue in which we should not want to participate!

One publication related seven things at the root of most gossip, calling them the "seven mischievous misses." They are: Misinformation, Misquotation, Misrepresentation, Misinterpretation, Misconception, Misconstruction, and Misunderstanding.[76] Take care never to get caught up in any of these!

Gossip is a sign that a person's consecration is waning. When a person begins to get spiritually empty, his speech often deteriorates. The words of Jesus prove this.

> **Matthew 12:34-35**
>
> *O generation of vipers, how can ye, being evil, speak good things? for out of the abundance of the heart the mouth speaketh. [35]A good man out of the good treasure of the heart bringeth forth good things: and an evil man out of the evil treasure bringeth forth evil things.*

- **Slander**

> **Psalm 101:5**
>
> *Whoso privily slandereth his neighbour, him will I cut off: him that hath an high look and a proud heart will not I suffer.*

There is a difference between gossip and slander. Gossip is not necessarily with the express purpose of doing harm. It may

---

[76] Griffin, Kelsey, Dan Segraves, Ralph Reynold, Rick Wyser, *Why? A Study of Christian Standards,* Word Aflame Publications. 1984.

cause harm, but many people tell things just for the thrill of telling them. Many love feeling as if they know something others don't.

On the other hand, slander is for the sole purpose of causing damage to someone else's character. This is extremely harmful since a person's most valuable asset is their reputation! Our reputation is more important than our net worth!

> **Proverbs 22:1**
> *A good name is rather to be chosen than great riches, and loving favour rather than silver and gold.*

Before you say something about someone else, ask yourself: (1) Is it kind? (2) Are you confident it is true? (3) Is it necessary? Whatever you share about another person should meet all three standards. For example, it may not be kind, even if it's true. As long as we limit what we share to things that are kind, true, and necessary, we will never have to worry about hurting someone else with our words.

You may have never considered this before, but when you bring an accusation against a brother or sister, you do the devil's job for him. Remember, he is the accuser of the brethren.

> **Revelation 12:10**
> *And I heard a loud voice saying in heaven, Now is come salvation, and strength, and the kingdom of our God, and the power of his Christ: for the accuser of our brethren is cast down, which accused them before our God day and night.*

There is another dimension to this sin that makes it even worse. Whether you help or hurt a brother, it is done as unto God.

> **Matthew 25:34-45**
> *Then shall the King say unto them on his right hand, Come, ye blessed of my Father, inherit the kingdom prepared for you from the foundation of*

the world: *35For I was an hungred, and ye gave me meat: I was thirsty, and ye gave me drink: I was a stranger, and ye took me in: 36Naked, and ye clothed me: I was sick, and ye visited me: I was in prison, and ye came unto me. 37Then shall the righteous answer him, saying, Lord, when saw we thee an hungred, and fed thee? or thirsty, and gave thee drink? 38When saw we thee a stranger, and took thee in? or naked, and clothed thee? 39Or when saw we thee sick, or in prison, and came unto thee? 40And the King shall answer and say unto them, Verily I say unto you, Inasmuch as ye have done it unto one of the least of these my brethren, ye have done it unto me. 41Then shall he say also unto them on the left hand, Depart from me, ye cursed, into everlasting fire, prepared for the devil and his angels: 42For I was an hungred, and ye gave me no meat: I was thirsty, and ye gave me no drink: 43I was a stranger, and ye took me not in: naked, and ye clothed me not: sick, and in prison, and ye visited me not. 44Then shall they also answer him, saying, Lord, when saw we thee an hungred, or athirst, or a stranger, or naked, or sick, or in prison, and did not minister unto thee? 45Then shall he answer them, saying, Verily I say unto you, Inasmuch as ye did it not to one of the least of these, ye did it not to me.*

Paul was aware of this fact. Perhaps that is why he disfellowshipped two men who were guilty of slander.

1 Timothy 1:20

Of whom is Hymenaeus and Alexander; whom I have delivered unto Satan, that they may learn not to blaspheme.

The word "blaspheme" simply means to vilify or speak evil about someone or something. In this case, it is unclear who or what was being spoken against, but the point is that the only recorded time Paul took such drastic action against church members was when they failed to control their tongues!

Looking back at the Old Testament, God instructed Moses on how to deal with the problem of slander. The punishment was based on the accusation.

Deuteronomy 19:15-21

One witness shall not rise up against a man for any iniquity, or for any sin, in any sin that he sinneth: at the mouth of two witnesses, or at the mouth of three witnesses, shall the matter be established. [16]If a false witness rise up against any man to testify against him that which is wrong; [17]Then both the men, between whom the controversy is, shall stand before the LORD, before the priests and the judges, which shall be in those days; [18]And the judges shall make diligent inquisition: and, behold, if the witness be a false witness, and hath testified falsely against his brother; [19]Then shall ye do unto him, as he had thought to have done unto his brother: so shalt thou put the evil away from among you. [20]And those which remain shall hear, and fear, and shall henceforth commit no more any such evil among you. [21]And thine eye shall not pity; but life shall go for life, eye for eye, tooth for tooth, hand for hand, foot for foot.

Under the law, if one person accused someone else and was found to be making a false accusation, the accuser was to suffer whatever punishment would have befallen the accused had he been found guilty. To clarify, suppose Person A accused Person B of murder. Once the matter was investigated, if Person B (the accused) were found innocent, Person A (the accuser) would receive the punishment prescribed for the accusation. In this case, someone guilty of gossip would receive the death penalty (the punishment for murder). There is no question such a law would significantly reduce the temptation to accuse anyone of anything!

Controlling our tongue is not an option. Yet, as James pointed out, it is not humanly possible for us to do so. Therefore, it is incumbent on us to seek God's help, asking Him to do what we cannot. Perhaps each of us should pray the same prayers David prayed with regard to our words.

Psalm 141:3
Set a watch, O LORD, before my mouth; keep the door of my lips.

Psalm 19:14
Let the words of my mouth, and the meditation of my heart, be acceptable in thy sight, O LORD, my strength, and my redeemer.

Guarding Your Tongue

GUARDING YOUR EYES

Matthew 6:22-23
The light of the body is the eye: if therefore thine eye be single, thy whole body shall be full of light. 23But if thine eye be evil, thy whole body shall be full of darkness. If therefore the light that is in thee be darkness, how great is that darkness!

What did Jesus mean when He spoke of our eye being "single"? *Barnes' Notes* says the phrase indicates our attention is "directed to one object."[77] If we want the fullness of God's light to shine within us and through us, our eye must be single. We must be looking only to one purpose – not to both God AND the world.

Matthew 6:33
But seek ye first the kingdom of God, and his righteousness; and all these things shall be added unto you.

When someone speaks of doing something "first," we generally expect at least one other thing to follow. Please notice, however, that there is nothing we are to "seek second." If we seek God's Kingdom, we have no reason to look for anything else.

---

[77] Barnes, A., J. G. Murphy, F. C. Cook, E. B. Pusey, H.C. Leupold, & R. Frew, *Barnes' Notes*. Blackie & Son, 1847.

The idea Jesus is conveying is not that God's Kingdom is number one on the list. Rather, He is saying God's Kingdom IS the list. Nothing else should be allowed to vie for our attention.

Just as we must strive diligently to control our tongues, so we must work equally as hard to control the things at which we allow ourselves to look. The reason for this is because the eye affects the heart.

> **Lamentations 3:51**
> Mine eye affecteth mine heart because of all the daughters of my city.

When we allow our eyes to view something, it opens a gateway to our heart. What is in the heart then governs our actions.

> **Proverbs 23:7**
> For as he thinketh in his heart, so is he: Eat and drink, saith he to thee; but his heart is not with thee.

Thus, the eye determines what we end up doing. There is great potential that you will become what you allow yourself to see! In his book *Practical Holiness*, David Bernard writes, "The eye is the primary means by which external information enters the mind, thereby stimulating our thought life."[78]

In 1969, Edgar Dale (an American Educator) created something he called the "Cone of Experience." Based on his studies, he concluded that we retain three times as much of what we see as opposed to what we hear.[79] Whether this is entirely accurate has been debated. Nevertheless, there is little question

---

[78] Bernard, David K., *Practical Holiness: A Second Look*, Word Aflame Press, 1985.

[79] Dupont, Laurent, Research Gate, https://www.researchgate.net/figure/Edgar-Dale-Audio-Visual-Methods-in-Teaching-3rd-Edition-Holt-Rinehart-and-Winston_fig1_283011989

that the eye is the "window of the soul." Through it pass the things which eventually enter into your heart.

What gets into your heart is what ultimately defiles (or justifies) you. Jesus explained this to His disciples.

Mark 7:20-23
And he said, That which cometh out of the man, that defileth the man. ^{21}For from within, out of the heart of men, proceed evil thoughts, adulteries, fornications, murders, ^{22}Thefts, covetousness, wickedness, deceit, lasciviousness, an evil eye, blasphemy, pride, foolishness: ^{23}All these evil things come from within, and defile the man.

John said there are only three ways the world can entice us. It could be said, therefore, that approximately 1/3 of all the world has to offer comes through the eye.

1 John 2:16
For all that is in the world, the lust of the flesh, and the lust of the eyes, and the pride of life, is not of the Father, but is of the world.

Peter spoke of people who were self-willed. He said they have "<u>eyes</u> full of adultery."

2 Peter 2:14
Having eyes full of adultery, and that cannot cease from sin; beguiling unstable souls: an heart they have exercised with covetous practices; cursed children:

We must take control over what we see. Job was identified as a "perfect" man (Job 1:1). I believe part of what qualified him for such a noble classification was the fact he had control over what he allowed himself to view.

> **Job 31:1**
> *I made a covenant with mine eyes; why then should I think upon a maid?*

David taught an important lesson concerning the things we look at. Consider his description of how he determined to live.

> **Psalm 101:4-7**
> *A froward heart shall depart from me: I will not know a wicked person. ⁵Whoso privily slandereth his neighbour, him will I cut off: him that hath an high look and a proud heart will not I suffer. ⁶Mine eyes shall be upon the faithful of the land, that they may dwell with me: he that walketh in a perfect way, he shall serve me. ⁷He that worketh deceit shall not dwell within my house: he that telleth lies shall not tarry in my sight.*

In this passage, the Psalmist expressed concern about the things he allowed himself to see. This becomes even clearer when reading the two verses before his definition of "perfect behavior."

> **Psalm 101:2-3**
> *I will behave myself wisely in a perfect way. O when wilt thou come unto me? I will walk within my house with a perfect heart. ³I will set no wicked thing before mine eyes: I hate the work of them that turn aside; it shall not cleave to me.*

Notice that David said, "I will SET no wicked thing before mine eyes." He realized he could not help some things he saw, but he determined he would not CHOOSE to view anything wicked!

I have often cautioned people about controlling what they see. In response, some people have argued, "You see the same things at the mall." My answer to them is straightforward. I tell them, "I can't choose what I HAVE to see when shopping for necessities. I can choose, however, ***NOT TO BRING THOSE***

THINGS INTO THE SANCTUARY OF MY HOME!

I am not able to avoid seeing some things which are ungodly. However, when I get on a computer, cell phone, or tablet (or any other device) or pick up a publication, book, or picture, I am making a willful choice as to what I am seeing.

Before going any further, it would help to get a better understanding of just how dangerous it is for us to look at some things. In order to do so, I need to spend some time explaining a special category of sin called "abominations."

An abomination is something that is utterly detestable. It is something to be hated with EXTREME abhorrence. The connotation is that the thing in question causes a hatred so intense it makes the person sick even to consider it.

Knowing this, it is astounding to realize God finds some practices and actions "abominable." This is astounding because although God IS love (1 John 4:8), there are some things He hates so much they make Him sick!

While God hates all sin, anything classified as "an abomination unto God" (such as in Deuteronomy 22:5) seems to be on a level far beyond just any sin. Because of this fact, it would be fitting to examine what God hates so intensely.

By and large, the transgressions which are called abominations can be grouped into six categories.[80] We will identify each category, along with some of the sins that fit within that group.

- **Moral Abominations**

Generally, these involve sexual sins like homosexuality (Leviticus 18:22) and bestiality (Leviticus 18:23). However, this

---

[80] Griffin, Kelsey, Dan Segraves, Ralph Reynold, Rick Wyser, *Why? A Study of Christian Standards,* Word Aflame Publications. 1984.

can include other things that involve immoral actions, attitudes, or even thoughts. Two examples are evil imaginations (Proverbs 6:16-19) and dressing in a way that represents the opposite sex (Deuteronomy 22:5). There are many others as well.

- **Occult Abominations**

This category involves practices which rely on powers that do not glorify God. In this group would be things like divination, observing the times, enchantment, witchcraft, familiar spirits, wizardry, and necromancy (Deuteronomy 18:9-14).

- **Vocal Abominations**

Within this group are the abuses of the human tongue. This includes, but is not limited to: Lying, bearing false witness, and sowing discord (Proverbs 6:16-19), and justifying the wicked and condemning the just (Proverbs 17:15).

- **Abominations of Worship**

This category includes the worship of objects, whether animate or inanimate, other than God. It also includes acts involving improper worship and service to the true God of Heaven. Among these are things like idolatry (Deuteronomy 7:25), sacrificing to God less than the best (Deuteronomy 17:1), the sacrifices of a wicked person (Proverbs 15:8), praying yet refusing to hear the Word of God (Proverbs 28:9), and offering to God money made from sinful practices (Deuteronomy 23:18).

- **Abominations of Character**

These are wicked acts that are the result of having a corrupt inward man. This would be things involving a man's attitude, outlook, motives, and behavior, such as: frowardness *[deviousness, crookedness, perverseness]* (Proverbs 3:32), pride and being quick to run to mischief (Proverbs 6:16-18), and following the way of the wicked (Proverbs 15:9).

- **Violent Abominations**

This describes various attacks against the sacredness of human life. Within this category would be murder (Proverbs 6:16-17) and abortion (Exodus 21:22-25).

What, then, should be our attitude toward abominations? To answer this question, the first important factor we must consider is that the essential nature of God is unchanging.

Malachi 3:6
For I am the LORD, I change not; therefore ye sons of Jacob are not consumed.

The things that pleased Him yesterday please Him today, and they will please Him tomorrow. Things which displeased Him yesterday displease Him today, and so will they tomorrow.

If something displeases God, it does so because of its destructive nature. He desires His children to have abundant life, and He knows certain things are destructive and deadly. For this reason, we can safely conclude that once something has been called an abomination to God, it will always be an abomination.

Remember, the definition of an abomination is something God loathes, hates, detests. He looks upon it as morally disgusting. It makes God "sick to His stomach."

I ask again, how are we to feel about those things which are an abomination to God? The answer should be clear – we must abhor, avoid, and take whatever steps are necessary to cut ourselves off from that which displeases the Lord. We must refuse to allow destructive elements to influence us in any way!

Deuteronomy 7:26
Neither shalt thou bring an abomination into thine house, lest thou be a cursed thing like it: but thou shalt utterly detest it, and thou shalt utterly abhor it; for it is a cursed thing.

While the context of this verse deals with idols, the principle extends to anything that is an abomination. Based on that understanding of Deuteronomy 7:26, I want to offer three principles about abominations of which we should be aware.

1. **It is forbidden to bring an abomination into one's home.** The abominable thing influences members of the family and corrupts them. They will begin taking on the characteristics associated with something God hates.

2. **That which is abominable is cursed.** Some things are blessed, while others are cursed. When one associates with that which is blessed or does things that are blessed, benefits accrue to him. (An example of this would be a sinner paying tithes and receiving financial blessings as a result.) When one associates with or does that which is cursed, however, he opens the door to negative influences, and the curse of God rests upon him.

3. **One's attitude towards an abomination should be utter hatred.** When it is clearly determined a thing or practice is an abomination, one's hatred of it should cause him to separate himself from it totally. His attitude will motivate him not to want any association with it at all.

2 Corinthians 6:17
Wherefore come out from among them, and be ye separate, saith the Lord, and touch not the unclean thing; and I will receive you,

It may seem irrelevant to the title of this chapter ("Guarding Your Eyes"), but there is a reason I have taken so much time to address the subject of abominations. It is because of the constant barrage of abominations that are streamed before our eyes electronically. Nowhere is this more true than on television and in movies.

When it comes to TV, nothing about the metal, plastic, wood, glass, or wiring is abominable. The overwhelming majority of programming, on the other hand, is.

In the same way, paper, ink, and glue are not abominable. Nevertheless, some books contain abominations.

A camera and film (or a printing press) are not abominable. They can, however, be used to create abominations.

I want to clearly state it is not the technology that is sinful. It is the images and messages which are transmitted that portray limitless abominations.

In fact, all six categories of abominations are openly displayed – AND PROMOTED – in movies, videos, and television programs. Scripturally, just because you don't actively participate in an abomination doesn't mean you're not under condemnation. The Apostle Paul warned not only about those who are involved but also those who derive pleasure from observing them!

Romans 1:32
Who knowing the judgment of God, that they which commit such things are worthy of death, not only do the same, but have pleasure in them that do them.

Early in this chapter, I pointed out how what you see affects what you eventually become. It is for this reason we should not watch anything that will have a negative impact on our spiritual condition. Let me be clear: it is not JUST television. This applies to ANY method of delivery which "sets" something wicked "before our eyes."

The impact of television has been unquestionably established. For example, "Teenagers who watch a lot of television with sexual content are twice as likely to engage in intercourse than those who watch few such programs, according to a study published today."[81] This article goes on to say, "The impact of television viewing is so large that even a moderate shift in the sexual content of adolescent TV watching could have a substantial effect on their sexual behaviour."[82]

As far back as 1985, Assembly of God preacher David Wilkerson put together a list of principles concerning the evils of television. He called it "31 Scriptural Reasons Why Overcoming Christians Should Remove the Idol of Television From their Homes."[83] While I cannot condone everything the man wrote, he definitely got it right about TV.

He wrote, "The world is about to burn and its foundations shaken by the almighty hand of God, and Christians sit nonchalantly before their television idol, wasting precious time. How Satan and the hoards of hell must laugh with glee at the sight of millions of Christians sitting before his Babylonian idiot box, losing their zeal for God.

"Satan is succeeding through television in a way not possible by any other kind of demonic invasion. Through that speaking idol, he can accomplish in this generation what he accomplished in Eden. He once again is tempting and enticing with the same three seductions: pride of life, lust of the eyes, and lust of the flesh. Television makes all three seductions possible.

"Twenty-five years ago television was rather innocent and harmless. There was wholesome family entertainment, and high moral standards were honored. Each broadcasting day was closed with a sermonette and a prayer. ... In the past few years that has all changed, and television is now not innocent, not wholesome,

---

[81] Conlon, Michael, Reuters, *TV and Other Factors Lead to Early Teen Sex: Study,* https://www.reuters.com/article/lifestyle/tv-and-other-factors-lead-to-early-teen-sex-study-idUSTRE4AO049, November 24, 2008.

[82] *Ibid.*

[83] Wilkerson, David, *Set the Trumpet to Thy Mouth,* Sovereign World Publishers, 1985.

and not worthy of the moral standard of a devoted lover of the Lord Jesus Christ.

"By the time a teenager is 18, he has watched an equivalent of 6 years of television and had only 4 months of church. And people tell me it's not an idol."[84]

There are, sadly, those who justify having a television by claiming there is no difference between TV and the internet. To begin with, if that is REALLY the case, they should get rid of their internet, too!

Beyond that, there IS a difference. In fact, there is more in common between the internet and a library than between the internet and a TV. A library contains a vast spectrum of literature. Much of it can be extremely helpful. In many libraries, there are also books which are pornographic in nature. The library itself is not "evil," but certain areas on the premises are. It all depends on the choices one makes while in that facility.

A person could spend an entire day in the library and never once encounter images of a sexual nature. The flip side is that someone who goes there LOOKING for filthy material can spend the entire day in the same building and ONLY see ungodliness and perversion.

The internet is nothing more or less than an electronic library. As long as I stay away from the wicked "areas," the internet can be most beneficial.

With a television (or in a movie theater, for that matter), it is a much different picture (pun intended). The only "choices" the viewer has are between what various ungodly producers or program directors are providing.

Perhaps the best explanation I have heard was an analogy I heard a man use a few years ago. Suppose you went into an "all-

---

[84] Wilkerson, David, *Set the Trumpet to Thy Mouth,* Sovereign World Publishers, 1985.

you-can-eat buffet." Upon arrival, you see two buffet tables. One is filled with garbage and filth, with the occasional "good food" item here and there. The other is filled with even WORSE garbage and filth, but also contains some of the most healthy food items available. The REAL difference is that, with the first table (which had almost NO "good" items), someone is standing behind the table, controlling what goes on your plate. On the other, you are given the utensils to help your OWN plate. In that line, YOU choose what goes on the plate and what you refuse. THAT, my friends, is the difference between the internet and television. With TV, Hollywood controls the serving utensils!

Although many Apostolic churches still preach against television and movie theaters, some members within those churches have found alternative methods to watch the exact same content. What good does it do to abstain from going to a theater if we bring the same movie into our home via computer, cell phone, or other electronic device?

Long before the advent of television, holiness churches were preaching against viewing ungodly movies. In fact, even before there WERE movies, holiness churches were preaching against viewing ungodly plays and dramas. I contend that the technology matters little. A separated people will refrain from unwholesome content.

In *Practical Holiness*, David Bernard writes, "New technological advances ... confront us with new situations. [Some people may] see the possibility of harmless and even beneficial use. However, whatever is objectionable at the movie theater or on television is certainly objectionable on these systems. Therefore, we must reject the showing of Hollywood movies."[85]

He continues, "In some cases, families that do not view

---

[85] Bernard, David K., *Practical Holiness: A Second Look,* Word Aflame Press, 1985.

movies or TV have allowed a worldly spirit to enter their homes through video. This can become a great danger to the church. ... We should view only those things that are clearly compatible with the Christian lifestyle, such as recordings of family and church activities and videos for teaching and business."[86]

Personally, I see video as the devil's alternative to cause people to start watching what they once refused to watch. It is possible right now to watch practically ANY Hollywood movie on our computers, tablets, and smartphones. Should we preach against those devices also? I do not believe that is the answer.

I believe we should continue to preach against television. There is no redeeming value in it and absolutely NO reason a Christian should have – or WANT – one. I also believe we should be consistent in denouncing ungodly content regardless of the technology involved.

Biblical principles will HAVE to be our guide. Don't allow yourself to find pleasure in unwholesome, ungodly, and/or abominable practices. Don't bring abominations into your home. Make a covenant with your eyes.

Here are some commitments I recommend you make concerning abominations:

    1. **I will abstain from personally committing abominations.**

    2. **I will cleanse our home of all abominations.**

    3. **I will refuse to permit abominable persons to influence our homes.**

    4. **I will refuse to be entertained by abominable practices, whether through viewing them, reading about them, or listening to them.**

---

[86] Bernard, David K., *Practical Holiness: A Second Look,* Word Aflame Press, 1985.

Those who still stand faithfully against the evil influence of television and unwholesome movies should be grateful to God for being spared the devastating influence of evil which these things bring upon us. Only eternity will reveal how many homes have stayed together, how many children have been spared from losing their faith in God, and how many churches have prospered to win souls all as a result of the decision to guard our eyes – the window of the soul.

GUARDING AGAINST IMMORALITY

Proverbs 2:11-19

Discretion shall preserve thee, understanding shall keep thee: ^{12}To deliver thee from the way of the evil man, from the man that speaketh froward things; ^{13}Who leave the paths of uprightness, to walk in the ways of darkness; ^{14}Who rejoice to do evil, and delight in the frowardness of the wicked; ^{15}Whose ways are crooked, and they froward in their paths: ^{16}To deliver thee from the strange woman, even from the stranger which flattereth with her words; ^{17}Which forsaketh the guide of her youth, and forgetteth the covenant of her God. ^{18}For her house inclineth unto death, and her paths unto the dead. ^{19}None that go unto her return again, neither take they hold of the paths of life.

The subject of this chapter is a delicate one. It is one which some Apostolic leaders do not feel comfortable addressing. I will do my best to be discreet in my approach to this topic. Nevertheless, I am firmly convinced it needs to be addressed now, more than ever before! Sadly, there is a tidal wave of ungodly sexual activity sweeping through our world, and conservative churches are not exempt.

Guarding Against Immorality

When it comes to acts of sexual immorality, the first thing we should recognize is this is much more than "just another sin." Like all sins (except blasphemy against the Holy Ghost), moral failure can be forgiven. Unlike the others, this has a pronounced lifelong aftereffect.

> **Proverbs 6:32-33**
> *But whoso committeth adultery with a woman lacketh understanding: he that doeth it destroyeth his own soul. [33]A wound and dishonour shall he get; and his reproach shall not be wiped away.*

Adultery brings a lasting reproach that cannot be removed. Many other translations use the word "disgrace" instead of "reproach." The writer is saying that, although the sin can be forgiven, there are lasting emotional scars and other consequences that will never be fully removed.

The pain, devastation, grief, and shame associated with this sin go far beyond the heart of the one committing it. We will discuss this in more detail at a later point.

> **Proverbs 2:18-19**
> *For her house inclineth unto death, and her paths unto the dead. [19]None that go unto her return again, neither take they hold of the paths of life.*

Again, no one ever fully recovers from this devastation. They will never be the same person they were prior to their immorality!

Proverbs 7 tells the story of a young man "void of understanding" who succumbs to the lure of an ungodly woman, yielding to the lust of his flesh. To conclude the story, Solomon described the tragic result of this moment of self-gratification.

> **Proverbs 7:22-27**
> *He goeth after her straightway, as an ox goeth to the slaughter, or as a fool to the correction of*

the stocks; *²³Till a dart strike through his liver; as a bird hasteth to the snare, and knoweth not that it is for his life. ²⁴Hearken unto me now therefore, O ye children, and attend to the words of my mouth. ²⁵Let not thine heart decline to her ways, go not astray in her paths. ²⁶For she hath cast down many wounded: yea, many strong men have been slain by her. ²⁷Her house is the way to hell, going down to the chambers of death.*

Another way to translate the word "chambers" is "darkest vaults." Another meaning of "death" (as it is used here) is "ruin." *The Riggen Revised Version*[87] would read: "Her house is the way to hell, going down to the darkest vaults of ruin."

More than half a century of serving God has allowed me to see a clear pattern. If a spirit of immorality ever makes an in-road into a church, the result can literally shut down the assembly.

From what I've been told, a major denomination was ready to accept the Pentecostal message many years ago. They discovered, however, that the prominent Pentecostal leader working with them was guilty of immorality. This one man's infidelity impacted them so negatively that it drove them away as a movement. They no longer wanted any association with anything bearing the name "Pentecostal."

Because the results are so devastating, the enemy will do his best to attack every truth-preaching assembly in the area of immorality. The good people of God must fight this spirit with all they have if they want their church to succeed.

The only way a church can be victorious is if THE

---

[87] For those unfamiliar with my writings, this is a term I use when I offer what I believe to be a more clear expression of a verse of Scripture. I base these renditions on my understanding of the original language and the input of scholars. No actual book exists by this title.

INDIVIDUAL SAINTS conquer that spirit once and for all. Those who will not conquer it will ultimately lose out with God.

Do NOT fall into the trap of saying, "It could never happen to me or my family." That's what the devil wants you to think, so you'll drop your guard.

There are numerous Scriptures I could use to prove the sinfulness of various individual acts. Instead, I want to use these pages to provide some principles to assist you in this fight.

Before addressing those principles, I want to address what may be one of the most dangerous times in the life of a young person. It is when they begin "dating" (or "courting" – depending on the guidelines of the local church) that they face the greatest potential of succumbing to a spirit of immorality.

I will offer some thoughts on this subject with the caveat that every saint should follow the teachings of their pastor. He knows what is best for the local flock, and my opinions are not intended to usurp (or even question) his authority.

In my opinion, "Dating" for Christians should NOT be "recreational." It should be for the purpose of finding a mate. I would suggest that if you can't imagine you would ever marry them, you shouldn't "go out" with them in the first place!

Furthermore, if a young man can't support a wife, it's probably not wise to start dating/courting a young lady. Get your house in order before you try to bring someone else into it!

The other side of this equation is just as true. A young lady who cannot keep her room clean or show other signs of responsibility doesn't need to be dating/courting a young man.

By the way, one of the worst things a young person can do is to decide they are interested in someone without FIRST talking to their pastor! Many times, a young person's emotions get involved BEFORE seeking spiritual input. Then, their heart is broken (or they choose to disobey) if their pastor has to inform them he doesn't feel good about the relationship going forward.

It is highly likely the pastor knows things (or feels things) about an individual of which the interested party has no clue. Seeking the pastor's guidance prior to pursuing a relationship is for your own safety.

Furthermore, young people should seek the input and consent of their parents. This is especially true if the parents are in the church. (See Ephesians 6:1.)

To the parents reading this book, you are ultimately responsible for enforcing your church's guidelines, whatever they may be. I highly recommend you have a conference with your children to discuss the rules and guidelines. Then, make sure those rules are enforced within your home.

Having said that, let me now move on to some specific Biblical principles that will help to protect you from acts (and the spirit) of immorality. Although they are not deeply profound, they are essential.

- **Love God.**

This should be self-evident, but it is worth taking the time to state. Above all else, you must develop a deep, thorough, and lasting love for Jesus Christ.

> **Mark 12:30**
> *And thou shalt love the Lord thy God with all thy heart, and with all thy soul, and with all thy mind, and with all thy strength: this is the first commandment.*

A love for God will help you strive to please Him at all times in every way. His power is strong enough to keep you, no matter how overwhelming the temptation may be.

> **Jude 1:24**
> *Now unto him that is able to keep you from falling, and to present you faultless before the presence of his glory with exceeding joy,*

When Joseph was a slave in Egypt and faced temptation, he had no family or friends to guide him or assist him. Furthermore, there was no spiritual authority over him from whom he might fear reprimand. The only thing that kept him in the hour of testing was his love for God.

> ***Genesis 39:7-9***
> *And it came to pass after these things, that his master's wife cast her eyes upon Joseph; and she said, Lie with me. ⁸But he refused, and said unto his master's wife, Behold, my master wotteth not what is with me in the house, and he hath committed all that he hath to my hand; ⁹There is none greater in this house than I; neither hath he kept back any thing from me but thee, because thou art his wife: how then can I do this great wickedness, and sin against God?*

- **Use the Word.**

There is power in the Word of God. Memorizing and quoting verses can provide protection when your flesh, the devil, or the world tries to lead you astray. The Psalmist David addressed this fact.

> ***Psalm 119:11***
> *Thy word have I hid in mine heart, that I might not sin against thee.*

When you read about the temptation of Jesus in the wilderness, you see He used the Word against Satan during His temptation. Every time the devil offered Him an opportunity to do wrong, the Lord's response was to quote the Scripture. (See Matthew 4:1-14.)

Below, I offer a sampling of verses that can be helpful in times of temptation. It would be good to put these and *any other* pertinent scriptures <u>in your heart</u>. Read them, learn them, recite them, so you might not sin against God.

1 Chronicles 4:10
And Jabez called on the God of Israel, saying, Oh that thou wouldest bless me indeed, and enlarge my coast, and that thine hand might be with me, **and that thou wouldest keep me from evil**, that it may not grieve me! And God granted him that which he requested.

Matthew 6:13
And lead us not into temptation, but deliver us from evil: For thine is the kingdom, and the power, and the glory, for ever. Amen.

Proverbs 2:16-18
To deliver thee from the strange woman, even from the stranger which flattereth with her words; [17]Which forsaketh the guide of her youth, and forgetteth the covenant of her God. [18]For her house inclineth unto death, and her paths unto the dead.

There are obviously MANY other scriptures I could share. I will not take the time to write them all out, but I will mention a few from the Book of Proverbs: 2:19-20, 5:1-23, 6:24-35, 7:5-27, 9:13-18, 22:14, 23:26-28, and 30:20.

When you are facing temptation, there is an excellent passage to remember. It is found in Paul's first letter to the church in Corinth.

1 Corinthians 10:13
There hath no temptation taken you but such as is common to man: but God is faithful, who will not suffer you to be tempted above that ye are able; but will with the temptation also make a way to escape, that ye may be able to bear it.

The devil will often try to convince you that you are the only one who has ever faced this temptation. This verse lets us know it is actually common. It also assures us that God WILL help us escape if we just look to Him.

Another critical fact to remember about a time of temptation is that trials make you wiser, stronger, and better equipped to help others. God allows these things to come your way to reveal your weaknesses so He can deal with them. In this way, He purifies those who overcome when they are tempted.

> ***Job 23:10***
> *But he knoweth the way that I take: when he hath tried me, I shall come forth as gold.*

- ***Stay Busy for God!***

It was during an idle time when David committed adultery with Bathsheba. Rather than being on the battlefield where he belonged, he had chosen to stay home.

> ***2 Samuel 11:1***
> *And it came to pass, after the year was expired, at the time when kings go forth to battle, that David sent Joab, and his servants with him, and all Israel; and they destroyed the children of Ammon, and besieged Rabbah. But David tarried still at Jerusalem.*

When you are struggling with your flesh, immerse yourself in the work of God. Teach Bible Studies, encourage others – in other words, get outside of yourself and your problem. Don't let yourself become isolated and consumed.

- ***Maintain Your Integrity.***

> ***Proverbs 20:7***
> *The just man walketh in his integrity: his children are blessed after him.*

Integrity is doing right even when no one is looking! In every aspect of your life, you must determine to please God regardless of how difficult it may seem at the moment. If you begin to let down in one area, you weaken your resolve in every area. God has offered us "the breastplate of righteousness" (Ephesians 6:14) to protect our hearts against the wiles of the devil – and our flesh!

The Book of Genesis relates a situation in which Abimelech (a heathen king) was "withheld" from adultery. God said it was because He saw the integrity of the king's heart.

Genesis 20:6
And God said unto him in a dream, Yea, I know that thou didst this in the integrity of thy heart; for I also withheld thee from sinning against me: therefore suffered I thee not to touch her.

I am convinced God will provide supernatural strength to a person who lives a constant life of integrity. On the other hand, the Bible indicates a person can become so careless in their walk with God that He removes all restraint, allowing that individual to destroy themselves through acts of immorality.

Proverbs 22:14
The mouth of strange women is a deep pit: he that is abhorred of the LORD shall fall therein.

- **Use Your Mind.**

The Great Creator has endowed each of us with a most amazing – and powerful – tool: our mind. As mentioned in a previous chapter, our thoughts eventually determine our lifestyle. (See Proverbs 23:7.) With that being the case, the person who can "gird up the loins" of his mind (1 Peter 1:13) will be able to overcome the carnal desires warring against his soul.

Paul spoke of the power of our mind when dealing with the spiritual weapons of warfare provided to a Christian. He also told us exactly how to use that weapon.

> **2 Corinthians 10:4-5**
> *(For the weapons of our warfare are not carnal, but mighty through God to the pulling down of strong holds;) ⁵Casting down imaginations, and every high thing that exalteth itself against the knowledge of God, and bringing into captivity every thought to the obedience of Christ;*

When your thoughts begin to focus on ungodly things, you must be proactive. Notice the terminology Paul used: "Casting down" and "bringing into captivity." These are not passive concepts! EVERY THOUGHT must be brought "to the obedience of Christ!"

You CANNOT dwell on impure thoughts without them affecting your actions! Ralph Waldo Emerson said, "Sow a thought and you reap an action; sow an act and you reap a habit; sow a habit and you reap a character; sow a character and you reap a destiny."[88] It all begins with a thought.

This helps to establish just how dangerous pornography is. While there may be no physical act of fornication or adultery taking place, it is certainly happening in the mind of the viewer. It should be noted that, according to Scripture, God sees both the physical act and the mental thoughts as one and the same.

> **Matthew 5:28**
> *But I say unto you, That whosoever looketh on a woman to lust after her hath committed adultery with her already in his heart.*

It is impossible to stress strongly enough just how important it is to maintain control of our thoughts. Whatever you are going

---

[88] Emerson, Ralph Waldo, *Sow a Thought and You Reap an Action*, The Complete Works of Ralph Waldo Emerson, edited by Edward Waldo Emerson, vol. 2, Houghton, Mifflin and Company, 1883.

to allow your mind to dwell on, it should fit the criteria provided in the Book of Philippians.

> ***Philippians 4:8***
> *Finally, brethren, whatsoever things are true, whatsoever things are honest, whatsoever things are just, whatsoever things are pure, whatsoever things are lovely, whatsoever things are of good report; if there be any virtue, and if there be any praise, think on these things.*

Of course, our thoughts are often directed by the things we allow our eyes to see. Since I devoted an entire chapter to this, I will only remind you to be very careful what you "set before your eyes!" (See Psalm 101:3.)

One way to "take your thoughts captive" is to list the things you could lose if you give in to your flesh. Included in your list should be:

- Your soul (if you could not recover spiritually, and many don't)
- Your self-respect and the respect of others
- Your family and possibly their salvation
- If it is a co-worker, your job, and possibly any type of a decent future

While this is by no means a thorough list, it should help you weigh out the risks involved. When the temptation comes, review your list and cast down the imagination! Doing so will hopefully convince you that giving in is not worth the price you'll end up paying!

You can also make a list to remind you of the unbelievable damage, shame, grief, and pain that immorality would bring to: God, both families, the Church (*i.e.,* local damage), the Kingdom (*i.e.,* global damage), the Saints, your friends, sinners, yourself, and the person with whom you would commit the sin.

In the event you fall into immorality with someone who is not a member of the church, it is very likely they will never accept the truth. Your act of unrighteousness says to them there is really nothing to the saving and keeping power of God. They will probably believe the entire church is filled with hypocrites.

In such a situation, you could be guilty of ANOTHER tragedy: providing just cause for those outside God's Kingdom to speak evil of His people. This was precisely what the Lord said about David after he committed adultery.

> ***2 Samuel 12:14***
> *Howbeit, because by this deed thou hast given great occasion to the enemies of the LORD to blaspheme, the child also that is born unto thee shall surely die.*

There have been rare occasions when a sinner has gotten involved with someone who was supposed to be a Christian and did eventually come to God. Even when that happened, however, they undoubtedly had to live a tormented life of regret.

Earlier, I offered advice to single young people. Now, I would like to provide some guidance for married couples. What follows are some instructions uniquely applicable to those who are married. Adhering to the following precepts will offer a great deal of protection to your relationship.

- ***Love Your Spouse.***

Love is something that must constantly be renewed. It is foolish to think that just because we remain together, our love will remain as fresh as at the first if we don't actively work on our marriage.

After more than 40 years of pastoring, I could write a separate volume on this subject alone, but suffice it to say that whatever you did to win your spouse's affection initially, you should continue to do to maintain that affection.

Loving our wife or husband is not an option. It is commanded in the Scripture.

Ephesians 5:33
Nevertheless let every one of you in particular so love his wife even as himself; and the wife see that she reverence her husband.

You should strive to keep your marriage in as perfect a condition as possible. Here are a few things you can do to facilitate that goal:

- Use every negative situation as a format to build a better relationship.
- Learn from past mistakes so that you don't repeat them.
- Take time to pray specifically for God to put a deep love in your heart for your spouse.
- Keep working on good communication.
- Pray for wisdom and understanding for both you and your spouse.
- Take special time to be together.
- Listen to the inner radar that God has put in your spouse's heart to warn you of the wrong intentions of others.
- Be totally, and even painfully, honest with God, yourself, and your spouse concerning all your feelings and motives.
- However, once you talk to God about it, go on to other areas of prayer. Don't get swallowed up in the problem of self.
- Learn your spouse's emotional needs and work at meeting them.

Dr. Willard Harley says men and women generally have five basic "needs" in their lives, which, when fulfilled, will keep love fresh. According to his research, most women need: affection, conversation, honesty and openness, financial support, and family commitment. On the other hand, he said that men need: sexual fulfillment, recreational companionship, an attractive spouse, domestic support, and admiration. Dr. Harley maintains that if each spouse will focus on meeting at least two or three of these basic needs, their relationship will remain forever strong.[89]

Finally, let me offer a few personal principles which are good for everyone to follow. These suggestions can create a fence of protection around your life, helping you avoid the dangerous allure of carnal desires.

- **Establish Some Firm Principles that Will Govern Your Life.**

Set and keep a "Protection Plan" whereby it would be extremely difficult for you to fall. This plan should include:

- *Never be alone with a member of the opposite sex.* Whether it is in a car, a house, or even the church, it is always best to have someone else present.
- *Keep conversations directed towards proper decorum and minimum time.* Some things don't need to be discussed in mixed company – even if everyone is married! Furthermore, if you are married and want to compliment a person of the opposite sex, it is best to do so through the auspices of your spouse.
- *Refrain from "pats" and "hugs."* Sometimes, even a handshake can last too long. It is noteworthy that Paul said it is good not to even "touch" a woman – and yes, that word just means a literal touch! (See 1 Corinthians 7:1.)
- *Don't be flirtatious!* Someday, someone may take you up on your folly!
- *Be aware that your biggest enemy is your ego!* The Book of Proverbs connects harlotry with the act of flattery. (See Proverbs 2:16 and 7:5.) It is no coincidence that God's Word shows an immoral person to be a flatterer!

---

[89] Harley, Dr. Willard F., Jr., *His Needs, Her Needs,* Baker Publishing Group, 2011.

Your ego is not only dangerous when it comes to being proud, but it often becomes an even greater danger when someone is battling with inferiority! Either way, beware of those who appeal to your ego or take it upon themselves to meet emotional needs only God or your spouse should meet.

Red flags should go up anytime anyone offers comfort or understanding by berating or slandering your spouse, no matter how subtle it may seem. As someone once said, "Trust only your mother not to have a seductive motive up her sleeve."

Examine yourself for any sign of selfishness in you and do your best to kill it. The fact is most (if not all) moral sin stems from a root of selfishness.

o *Surround yourself with good friends.* The key word here is "good." Good friends inspire you to *do* good!

1 Corinthians 15:33
Be not deceived: evil communications corrupt good manners.

The *Bible in Basic English* says, "Do not be tricked by false words: evil company does damage to good behaviour."[90] The *English Standard Version* translates it, "Do not be deceived: 'Bad company ruins good morals.'"[91] The *Common English Bible* reads, "Don't fool yourselves. Bad friends will destroy you."[92]

o *Establish the fact that your pastor (or pastor's wife) is your only faithful confidant.* First, don't try to struggle through marital problems alone. The enemy thrives on the confusion and condemnation you feel. Having said that, I would also recommend you never discuss deep marital issues with another member of your congregation.

---

[90] Hooke, S. H., *The Bible in Basic English,* Cambridge University Press, 1982.
[91] *The Holy Bible: English Standard Version,* Crossway Books, 2001.
[92] *The Holy Bible: The Common English Bible,* Abingdon Press, 2011

Guarding Against Immorality

After the things necessary for survival (food, water, etc.), human sexuality can be the strongest drive a person ever experiences. Getting control in this area of our lives is absolutely essential. It is my sincere prayer that the simple suggestions I've presented in this chapter can help someone keep themselves "unspotted from the world" (James 1:27) and, in so doing, live a life of "sanctification and honor."

> ***1 Thessalonians 4:3-4***
> *For this is the will of God, even your sanctification, that ye should abstain from fornication: [4]That every one of you should know how to possess his vessel in sanctification and honour;*

OUTWARD ADORNING

1 Timothy 2:8-10
I will therefore that men pray every where, lifting up holy hands, without wrath and doubting. [9]In like manner also, that women adorn themselves in modest apparel, with shamefacedness and sobriety; not with broided hair, or gold, or pearls, or costly array; [10]But (which becometh women professing godliness) with good works.

In Chapter 3, I explained Scripturally how what we wear DOES matter to God. I addressed the statement "the Lord looketh on the heart" (1 Samuel 16:7), showing it has nothing to do with clothing and, therefore, cannot accurately be used to dispute the need for godly apparel.

I also showed how clothing mattered by dealing with the example of Adam and Eve (Genesis 3:21), Joshua the High Priest (Zechariah 3:3-5), and the demoniac of Gadara (Mark 5:15). I pointed out that the priests who served in the tabernacle were to dress first for glory and then for beauty (Exodus 28:2).

I then went on to show that New Testament writers also spoke on the subject of outward adorning. As examples, I cited Paul in 1 Timothy 2:8-10 and Peter in 1 Peter 3:3-5.

Having established this fact, I will use this chapter to deal with what the Bible says specifically about our outer appearance. My focus will be on three basic areas of adornment: clothing, cosmetics, and costly array.

- **Clothing**

Three important criteria should govern a Christian's clothing. Each of these is based on a Scriptural principle.

  o It must be modest.

   1 Timothy 2:9
   In like manner also, that women adorn themselves in modest apparel, with shamefacedness and sobriety; not with broided hair, or gold, or pearls, or costly array;

"Modest" and/or "modesty" can be defined in several ways. One meaning is "limited in size, amount, or scope."[93] This would signify the avoidance of extremes. For example, one might request a "modest" portion of food when being served. By that, they simply mean they do not want too much, nor do they want too little. In this case, the implication of the word is "in between."

The word "modesty" carries the connotation of humility. It is "freedom from vanity [or] boastfulness."[94] Another definition that is closely connected to this is "regard for decency."[95] Both of these imply "not given to pride or flirtation."

All of this gives us a proper understanding of what it means to wear "modest apparel." Using these definitions, we should be able to easily arrive at what the Biblical mandate means.

When God clothed Adam and Eve in the garden, He did so

---

[93] Merriam-Webster Dictionary, https://www.merriam-webster.com

[94] Dictionary.com, www.dictionary.com

[95] *Ibid.*

with the explicit intent of covering their nakedness. When we combine that fact with the definitions provided, we should have no problem establishing a "standard" of modesty.

To illustrate what I mean, consider our sleeve length. If we desire to have "modest" sleeves, we should first ask ourselves what we are trying to cover. Obviously, the answer is our arms. Therefore, if we want to be sure our sleeves are modest, we must (1) Cover anything that would be indecent, (2) Avoid appearing flirtatious, and (3) Set a length that at least covers the "in-between point" of the two ends of the arm (which would be the elbow).

It would stand to reason, then, that the bare minimum would be to cover the elbow. In doing so, however, one should consider the fact that the midpoint should be covered at all times – even during times of raising the hands or other forms of movement. This would lead me to believe the standard for sleeve length should be at some point below the elbow, which guarantees that the midpoint will never be publicly exposed.

The same pattern can be used for the length of a woman's skirt. In this case, it is the leg which is being covered. The halfway (or "in-between") point would be the knee. Making sure the skirt is long enough so the knee is never exposed (whether standing, sitting, or being active in any way) would be considered "modest."

I might add that having a hemline well beyond the knee does little good if the leg is exposed by a split in the skirt. A split might actually be more alluring than a skirt that would only be as long as where the top of the split begins. It can be argued that wearing a split draws more attention to the leg (which is supposed to be covered) and might suggest an invitation to look above the hem.

Necklines should be set at a point where the individual is decent from any angle. For instance, when a woman comes to the front for prayer, her pastor should not have to turn his head away because her neckline is so low (or hanging so loose) that looking at her is taking the risk of seeing more than he should!

Of course, a person can meet (or even exceed) any of these guidelines and still not be modest. If the garment he or she is wearing is too tight, it doesn't matter how long the sleeves or skirt might be or how high the neckline is. Clothing that is too clingy or form-fitting is still indecent.

Please allow me to interject something at this point. I want to stress again that I do not have the desire – nor the authority – to set a standard for any assembly other than the one over which God has placed me. That is not my intention.

All I want to do is provide some very basic guidelines that might help those with an honest heart who genuinely desire to know more about how they can please God. The reader should obey whatever guidelines your godly pastor has prayerfully and carefully set for your church under the auspices of the Word of God.

- o It must show a distinction between the sexes.

   Deuteronomy 22:5
   The woman shall not wear that which pertaineth unto a man, neither shall a man put on a woman's garment: for all that do so are abomination unto the LORD thy God.

In chapter 9, I spent several pages dealing with abominations. I not only explained what they are, but I showed that anything God has ever found abominable remains in that category to this day.

This is why we obey Deuteronomy 22:5 but do not believe other commands in the same chapter apply to us today. Things like wearing garments made from different materials or planting various kinds of seeds in the same plot of ground were requirements for the Jewish religion. This verse, on the other hand, plainly states wearing apparel associated with the opposite sex is an abomination unto God.

Looking at the verse closely, we see the Lord unequivocally stated that the clothing worn by men and women should be uniquely representative of the sex of the wearer. However, please pay attention to the exact wording God used.

He stated it is an abomination for the man to wear "a woman's garment." For the woman, on the other hand, God said it is an abomination for her to wear "that which pertaineth to a man." Thus, for the woman, it goes beyond simply what BELONGS to a man. She is prohibited from wearing anything that even PERTAINS to a man!

The word "pertain" means "to have reference or relation." There is no question that pants are related to men, and not just in the United States. This is true all around the world. I've been blessed to travel to many countries, and in every case, the distinction between the men's and ladies' restrooms was ALWAYS that the men's room had a sign with a figure wearing pants.

Regardless, the Bible makes a connection between pants and men. The first mention of pants is found in Exodus 28. The Lord instructed the priests to wear "linen breeches." Every other passage that mentions these "breeches" also describes the clothing for the priests – who were ALL men!

By using the word "pertain," God's prohibition goes beyond what was created for a man or intended for a man. If it in any way is RELATED to masculinity, a woman is committing an abomination if she wears it. This means one cannot claim, "These are women's pants," and think that excuses their practice.

It is very troubling that so many churches that once upheld this Scripture have started trying to explain it away. Rather than trying to make the Bible fit our lifestyle, we should adjust our lifestyle to fit the Bible! Even among some historically conservative churches, this concept has been relaxed and certain "exceptions" have been extended. This should not be.

If God considers something so loathsome it sickens Him, why would anyone think they could find some loophole permitting what is otherwise so unacceptable? Because God feels this way, it raises a higher level of concern than matters of simple modesty. I simply cannot imagine a scenario where a woman should be allowed to adorn herself in pants of any kind at any time! Nor should she be permitted to wear anything that would even look like pants to others.

- It must show a distinction between the world and the church.

    2 Corinthians 6:17-18
    Wherefore come out from among them, and be ye separate, saith the Lord, and touch not the unclean thing; and I will receive you, [18]And will be a Father unto you, and ye shall be my sons and daughters, saith the Lord Almighty.

It is incredible to me how many people who claim to be Christians want to follow every fad and fashion of this world. The Apostle Paul said it is only when we are separate from the world that God is willing to consider us His children. What a shame it is when some limp-wristed fashion designer in Paris has more effect on the church than an anointed man of God does!

We should not allow those outside the church to determine how we dress. Our guidebook is the Bible, not the latest trends. As the people of God, sinners ought to be able to recognize from a distance that we are unique.

Perhaps you are a new convert reading this book. If so, I urge you to look to your pastor and pastor's wife as the example, after which you can pattern yourself. Their clothing will clearly show what is expected of those born into the local church family.

Whether new converts or established saints, we should all thank God for the distinct look of Oneness Apostolics! It is a wonderful thing to have a "family resemblance" that clearly distinguishes us from the rest of the world.

- **Cosmetics**

Moving from the topic of clothing, it is imperative that we discuss the use of cosmetics. The Bible makes some clear statements regarding this subject. In 1 Timothy, Paul not only instructs women to dress modestly but also commands them to be "shamefaced."

1 Timothy 2:9-10

In like manner also, that women adorn themselves in modest apparel, with shamefacedness and sobriety; not with broided hair, or gold, or pearls, or costly array; [10]But (which becometh women professing godliness) with good works.

The word "shamefacedness" means bashfulness or modesty. The idea is to not wear anything on your face because of pride or flirtation.

The only reason a person would wear makeup would be either as a matter of pride or in an attempt to become "attractive" and appeal to the desires of another. Both of these reasons violate the parameters of "shamefacedness."

This is not just a matter of my personal opinion. The Bible makes a direct connection between cosmetics and the spirit of harlotry. One example is found in 2 Kings 9:30, where Jezebel "painted her face" in an attempt to entice Jehu.

Speaking through the Prophet Ezekiel, God referred to backslidden Israel as being "old in adulteries." To illustrate this, He said they had applied cosmetics and adorned themselves with jewelry.

Outward Adorning

> ### Ezekiel 23:40-43
> And furthermore, that ye have sent for men to come from far, unto whom a messenger was sent; and, lo, they came: for whom thou didst wash thyself, **paintedst thy eyes**, and deckedst thyself with ornaments, ⁴¹And satest upon a stately bed, and a table prepared before it, whereupon thou hast set mine incense and mine oil. ⁴²And a voice of a multitude being at ease was with her: and with the men of the common sort were brought Sabeans from the wilderness, which put bracelets upon their hands, and beautiful crowns upon their heads. ⁴³Then said I unto her that was old in adulteries, Will they now **commit whoredoms** with her, and she with them? [Emphasis added.]

Jeremiah addressed this same concept. He spoke of Israel's "lovers," saying the Jews had tried to entice them through wearing jewelry and applying makeup.

> ### Jeremiah 4:30
> And when **thou art spoiled**, what wilt thou do? Though thou clothest thyself with crimson, though thou deckest thee with ornaments of gold, though thou **rentest thy face with painting**, in vain shalt thou make thyself fair; **thy lovers** will despise thee, they will seek thy life. [Emphasis added.]

Early church leaders were outspoken in their opposition to the practice of wearing makeup. Tertullian, a theologian and apologist, wrote a book around 200 AD entitled "On the Apparel of Women." In it, he expressed strong opposition to women wearing cosmetics, viewing them as a form of vanity, deception, and moral corruption.[96]

Cyprian, who lived about 50 years after Tertullian, wrote a book entitled, "On the Dress of Virgins." His view was that cosmetics were a form of vanity that contradicted Christian modesty and spiritual beauty.[97]

Knowing what the Bible says – and what was the obvious practice within early Christianity – there should be a total abstinence from the use of cosmetics. Trying to change one's appearance through makeup, nail polish, hair dye, and such like is a clear sign that the wearer is dissatisfied with the way the Creator made you!

We are the clay. God is the potter. We should never be so presumptuous as to complain about how He designed our appearance.

Romans 9:20
Nay but, O man, who art thou that repliest against God? Shall the thing formed say to him that formed it, Why hast thou made me thus?

- **Costly Array**

Unfortunately, this topic is becoming more controversial than it has been during my lifetime. Like the subject of women wearing pants, many churches have begun making exceptions for wearing various types of "costly array." The two topics are also alike in that the Scripture offers a point-blank prohibition.

1 Timothy 2:9-10
In like manner also, that women adorn

---

[96] *The Ante-Nicene Fathers, Volume IV.* Alexander Roberts and James Donaldson, editors. W.B. Eerdmans Pub. Co, 1973.

[97] Cyprian, Saint, EWTN, *The Dress of Virgins,* https://www.ewtn.com/catholicism/library/dress-of-virgins-12507

> *themselves in modest apparel, with shamefacedness and sobriety; not with broided hair, or gold, or pearls, or costly array; ¹⁰But (which becometh women professing godliness) with good works.*

Thayer's Greek Lexicon says "costly" means "requiring great outlay, very costly."[98] *Vine's Expository Dictionary* says it means "of the highest cost."[99] *Strong's Exhaustive Concordance* explains it as "extremely expensive."[100]

The word "array" means "clothing" or "apparel." [101] It is a generic term for anything that is worn on the body.

Therefore, this verse requires Christians not to adorn themselves with any kind of clothing or apparel that is "extremely expensive." Because it is preceded by "gold" and "pearls," the phrase "costly array" is generally accepted as meaning the wearing of jewelry.

Although this will be the primary focus of our attention, it should still be noted the term is NOT limited to jewelry. In my opinion, therefore, Apostolic people should refrain from wearing ANYTHING that would be considered "extremely expensive" by the majority of those with whom they will come in contact.

As I mentioned, I will use the generally accepted

---

[98] Thayer, J., *A Greek-English Lexicon of the New Testament,* Baker Book House, 1993.

[99] Vine, W.E., J.R. Kohlenberger, J.A. Swanson, *The Expanded Vine's Expository Dictionary of New Testament Words.* Bethany House Publishers, 1984.

[100] Strong, James, *Strong's Exhaustive Concordance of the Bible,* Originally published 1890.

[101] Thayer, J., *A Greek-English Lexicon of the New Testament,* Baker Book House, 1993.

understanding of "costly array" for the remainder of this chapter. After all, it is astounding just how strongly the scripture prohibits the use of jewelry!

Like cosmetics, the Bible equates jewelry with sensual apparel and harlotry. The following Scriptures prove this to be the case.

Hosea 2:13
*And I will visit upon her the days of Baalim, wherein she burned incense to them, and she **decked herself with her earrings and her jewels**, and she **went after her lovers**, and forgat me, saith the LORD.* [Emphasis added.]

Ezekiel 23:40-43
*And furthermore, that ye have sent for men to come from far, unto whom a messenger was sent; and, lo, they came: for whom thou didst wash thyself, paintedst thy eyes, and **deckedst thyself with ornaments**, ⁴¹And satest upon a stately bed, and a table prepared before it, whereupon thou hast set mine incense and mine oil. ⁴²And a voice of a multitude being at ease was with her: and with the men of the common sort were brought Sabeans from the wilderness, which put **bracelets upon their hands**, and beautiful crowns upon their heads. ⁴³Then said I unto her that was old in adulteries, Will they now **commit whoredoms** with her, and she with them?* [Emphasis added.]

Jeremiah 4:30
*And when thou art spoiled, what wilt thou do? Though thou clothest thyself with crimson, though **thou deckest thee with ornaments of gold**, though thou rentest thy face with painting,*

in vain shalt thou make thyself fair; **_thy lovers_** *will despise thee, they will seek thy life.* [Emphasis added.]

Revelation 17:4-5

And the woman was arrayed in purple and scarlet colour, and **_decked with gold and_** *precious stones and pearls, having a golden cup in her hand full of abominations and filthiness of her fornication: ⁵And upon her forehead was a name written, MYSTERY, BABYLON THE GREAT,* **_THE MOTHER OF HARLOTS_** *AND ABOMINATIONS OF THE EARTH.* [Emphasis added.]

Besides identifying jewelry with immorality, the Bible also equates it with idolatry! This is clearly shown in the story of Jacob returning to Bethel.

After being instructed by God to build an altar, Jacob instructed his family to rid themselves of their "strange gods." He knew they could not find God's favor while practicing idolatry.

Genesis 35:2-5

Then Jacob said unto his household, and to all that were with him, Put away the strange gods that are among you, and be clean, and change your garments:

Jacob's family seemed to waste no time in obeying his directive. How they did so, however, is worth noting.

Genesis 35:4

And they gave unto Jacob all the strange gods which were in their hand, and all their earrings which were in their ears; and Jacob hid them under the oak which was by Shechem.

Understanding Separation

When told to get rid of the "strange gods," they responded by removing their earrings. Dr. Albert Barnes said that the phrase "strange gods which were in their hands" was a reference to "rings which were worn."[102] They recognized their jewelry as a form of idolatry!

The Prophet Isaiah made this connection as well. He spoke of "the ornament," which he identified as "thy molten images of gold." (See Isaiah 30:22.)

Jewelry associated is not only with harlotry and idolatry (which is bad enough). Jewelry is also equated with being "stiffnecked" (which means "stubborn").

Exodus 33:3-6
Unto a land flowing with milk and honey: for I will not go up in the midst of thee; for thou art a stiffnecked people: lest I consume thee in the way. ⁴And when the people heard these evil tidings, they mourned: and no man did put on him his ornaments. ⁵For the LORD had said unto Moses, Say unto the children of Israel, Ye are a stiffnecked people: I will come up into the midst of thee in a moment, and consume thee: therefore now put off thy ornaments from thee, that I may know what to do unto thee. ⁶And the children of Israel stripped themselves of their ornaments by the mount Horeb.

There is something worth noting in this passage. According to verse 4, "no man did put on him his ornaments." In verse 5, however, the Lord told them, "Put off thy ornaments." While this may sound confusing (if not contradictory) in our English Bible,

---

[102] Barnes, A., J. G. Murphy, F. C. Cook, E. B. Pusey, H.C. Leupold, & R. Frew, *Barnes' Notes*. Blackie & Son, 1847.

Outward Adorning

The Pulpit Commentary offers an explanation of what God actually said. "the word translated 'put off'... means 'lay aside altogether.' The intention was to make their continued disuse of the ornaments a test of their penitence."[103]

One possibility for why God is so opposed to jewelry may reside in the fact that, Scripturally, gold represents deity. For example, the Ark of the Covenant was to be made of wood, overlayed with gold. (See Exodus 25:10-11.)

Romans 3:25 calls Jesus our "propitiation." The Greek word used here only appears in one other passage. In Hebrews 9:5, the same word is translated as "mercy seat." It should be evident, then, that the Ark of the Covenant (for which the "mercy seat" was the covering) was a representation of the man Christ Jesus. The wood represents His humanity. The gold shows His deity.

Knowing gold is a symbol of deity helps us understand why Moses made the Israelites drink the gold from the melted calf. (See Exodus 32:19-20.) God wanted the gold to be on the INSIDE of His people!

Many years ago, I heard an evangelist say the Lord spoke to him about a lady as she walked by him. She was decked out in gold. God's words to him were something to the effect of, "The less gold a person has on the inside, the more they want it on the outside. The more gold a person has on the inside, the less they want it on the outside."

There is an undeniably strict prohibition against the wearing of gold in the Bible. God granted no exceptions!

1 Timothy 2:9-10
In like manner also, that women adorn themselves in modest apparel, with

---

[103] Spence-Jones, Henry Donald Maurice, and Joseph S. Exell, editors, *The Pulpit Commentary,* Funk & Wagnalls Company, 1890–1919.

> *shamefacedness and sobriety; not with broided hair, or gold, or pearls, or costly array; ¹⁰But (which becometh women professing godliness) with good works.*

When it comes to wearing jewelry, some people make an exception in the case of a wedding ring. Please note, however, that gold is forbidden even in the context of marriage!

1 Peter 3:1-5

> *Likewise, ye wives, be in subjection to your own husbands; that, if any obey not the word, they also may without the word be won by the conversation of the wives; ²While they behold your chaste conversation coupled with fear. ³Whose adorning let it not be that outward adorning of plaiting the hair, and of wearing of gold, or of putting on of apparel; ⁴But let it be the hidden man of the heart, in that which is not corruptible, even the ornament of a meek and quiet spirit, which is in the sight of God of great price. ⁵For after this manner in the old time the holy women also, who trusted in God, adorned themselves, being in subjection unto their own husbands:*

In this passage, Peter is specifically dealing with marriage relationships. It is in this context that the wife is commanded NOT to wear gold. He tells her the only "ornament" she needs is "a meek and quiet spirit."

Considering what Peter said, I will point out that the Bible DOES allow for some "ornaments." They are NOT jewelry, however. Other than the "meek and quiet spirit" Peter mentioned, there are two more: the instructions of those over you (Proverbs 1:7-9) and wisdom (Proverbs 4:7-9).

Wedding rings irrefutably originated in ancient Egypt. Considering that the first church (born in Jerusalem on the Day of Pentecost) – and all of the Apostles – consisted entirely of Jewish converts, it is beyond comprehension to think they would have permitted a custom tied to the original enemies of the Jewish people! That same attitude would have been handed down to the Gentile converts as they began coming into the church.

History is replete with sources proving that no Christian assembly permitted the use of wedding rings until 300-400 years after the church was founded. How is it, then, that modern Christians suddenly think it has become acceptable? They are certainly not allowing it on any Scriptural basis.

No doubt someone will ask about the ring given to the prodigal son. For that reason, let us closely examine the verse in question.

Luke 15:22
But the father said to his servants, Bring forth the best robe, and put it on him; and put a ring on his hand, and shoes on his feet:

Notice the ring was not placed on his finger but on his "hand." Based on the customs of first-century Israel, this would NOT have been an ornamental ring worn for fashion. Instead, it was a legal seal of authority made of clay and carried in a leather wrist pouch.

No matter how hard people may try, there simply is no Biblical example of wearing ornamental jewelry being discussed in a positive light. Even when it is not directly condemned, it is merely mentioned as something that happened. This does not show approval and should not be interpreted as though it does.

Whether we are talking about the clothes we put on, the use of cosmetics, or wearing costly array, we should always keep in mind that our lives are supposed to point people to the Savior. We should never be guilty of drawing attention to our flesh.

If you ever have the opportunity to visit a museum and view paintings created by various master artists, you might notice something they all have in common. None of the pictures are in elaborate frames. The frame is kept simple so as to keep the focus on the work of the "master."

When it comes to the child of God, Christ is the Picture. We are the frame. We should never wear anything that would cause the world to focus on the wrong one!

Outward Adorning

HAIR: THE LONG AND SHORT OF IT

1 Corinthians 11:13-16
Judge in yourselves: is it comely that a woman pray unto God uncovered? ¹⁴Doth not even nature itself teach you, that, if a man have long hair, it is a shame unto him? ¹⁵But if a woman have long hair, it is a glory to her: for her hair is given her for a covering. ¹⁶But if any man seem to be contentious, we have no such custom, neither the churches of God.

The Bible is a book filled with symbolic imagery. To fully comprehend what the Scriptures say about hair, it is important first to understand how significant these symbols are. To facilitate this process, we will consider a few examples.

In the previous chapter, I discussed how the Ark of the Covenant symbolized Jesus Christ. I should also note that the entire Tabernacle in the wilderness – and the procedures that took place there – represented Him as well. He was foreshadowed by the sacrifice (Hebrews 9:28) AND the altar (Hebrews 13:10) AND the High Priest (Hebrews 3:1)!

It is not enough to know that God used symbols, however. We should also realize how vital those symbols were in God's eyes. For example, when the Israelites journeying through the wilderness found themselves in need of water, an incident took place that would prove to be a symbol later used to portray Christ.

The first time this happened, God instructed Moses to smite a rock, promising to provide water for the people when he obeyed. (See Exodus 17:6.) Sometime later, they again found themselves needing water. This time, God told Moses to speak to a rock, and He would again supply the required hydration.

In this incident, however, Moses lashed out in anger and struck the rock instead of speaking to it. As a result, God pronounced severe punishment on him.

> **Numbers 20:12**
> *And the LORD spake unto Moses and Aaron, Because ye believed me not, to sanctify me in the eyes of the children of Israel, therefore ye shall not bring this congregation into the land which I have given them.*

Think about what this meant. At the end of 40 years of putting up with the complaints, doubts, fears, and rebellion of a multitude of people, he would not get to enjoy the benefits of the inheritance to which he was taking them. Why would God forbid Moses to enter the Promised Land simply because he hit a rock?

It would be ridiculous to think God was concerned about the literal rock. It felt nothing and knew nothing. The problem was not that a rock had been violated. The problem was a SYMBOL had been violated.

We know this from the writings of the Apostle Paul. According to him, the rock in the wilderness that provided life-giving water represented Jesus Christ.

> **1 Corinthians 10:4**
> *And did all drink the same spiritual drink: for they drank of that spiritual Rock that followed them: and that Rock was Christ.*

During His ministry, Jesus had proclaimed, "If any man thirst, let him come unto me, and drink" (John 7:37). Years after His death, burial, and resurrection, He appeared in a vision to the Apostle John and said, "I will give unto him that is athirst of the fountain of the water of life freely" (Revelation 21:6). The water Christ offers is available to us because He was smitten at Calvary.

Thus, the smiting of the rock in Exodus was intended to symbolize the provision made by Christ's death. However, Christ was only smitten once. After that, we can simply speak to Him and He will supply our needs. So when Moses smote the rock the second time, he broke the symbolism. That was the thing that aroused the anger of God. When He establishes a symbol, He expects all of humanity to reverence and respect that symbol.

This is not just an Old Testament principle. We see the same concept upheld through the observance of what we call "the Lord's Supper" or communion.

1 Corinthians 11:23-26

For I have received of the Lord that which also I delivered unto you, That the Lord Jesus the same night in which he was betrayed took bread: 24And when he had given thanks, he brake it, and said, Take, eat: this is my body, which is broken for you: this do in remembrance of me. 25After the same manner also he took the cup, when he had supped, saying, This cup is the new testament in my blood: this do ye, as oft as ye drink it, in remembrance of me. 26For as often as ye eat this bread, and drink this cup, ye do shew the Lord's death till he come.

When Jesus began this practice with His disciples, He established a lasting symbolism. The broken bread represents His body. The liquid from "the fruit of the vine" (Matthew 26:28) represents His blood. Paul said these symbols would not change "till He come."

In this same chapter, the apostle implored the recipients of his epistle to make sure they treated those symbols properly. He even went so far as to say that failure to do so brings "damnation."

> **1 Corinthians 11:29-30**
> For he that eateth and drinketh unworthily, eateth and drinketh damnation to himself, not discerning the Lord's body. ^{30}For this cause many are weak and sickly among you, and many sleep.

It is not because the bread IS Christ's body and the drink IS Christ's blood. It is because they are the symbol of those things. We have an obligation to honor those symbols and treat them with the highest regard.

Besides the importance of symbols, there is another factor that must be taken into consideration in order to comprehend fully the subject of hair. We must understand the context of the verses addressing the matter. Although Paul wrote about hair in 1 Corinthians 11, that was NOT the main topic. Rather, this chapter is dealing with the subject of authority.

> **1 Corinthians 11:1-4**
> Be ye followers of me, even as I also am of Christ. ^{2}Now I praise you, brethren, that ye remember me in all things, and keep the ordinances, as I delivered them to you. ^{3}But I would have you know, that the head of every man is Christ; and the head of the woman is the man; and the head of Christ is God. ^{4}Every man praying or prophesying, having his head covered, dishonoureth his head.

Look at how the chapter opens. Verse 1 instructs the people

to follow Paul's example. Verse 2 speaks of his gratitude for their obedience to him. Verse 3 provides a "chain of command," which shows that EVERYBODY has a "head" (meaning an authority over them). Verses 4 and 5 mention practices that show dishonor to that authority. These verses set the stage for everything that will follow in chapter 11.

It is in this context that Paul brings up the issue of hair. He presents the case that the length of a person's hair is the God-ordained symbol of their submission to authority (or the lack thereof).

He says that a man who does not honor the symbol of hair length is "dishonoring" the authority over him. A careful reading of the following verses reveals that "having his head covered" means having "long hair."

> *1 Corinthians 11:4*
>
> *Every man praying or prophesying, having his head covered, dishonoureth his head.*
>
> *1 Corinthians 11:7*
>
> *For a man indeed ought not to cover his head, forasmuch as he is the image and glory of God: but the woman is the glory of the man.*
>
> *1 Corinthians 11:14*
>
> *Doth not even nature itself teach you, that, if a man have long hair, it is a shame unto him?*

Using the same symbolism, Paul also addresses the women. In that case, he writes, a woman must not have her head "uncovered," which he explains is the result of willfully shortening her hair.

> *1 Corinthians 11:5-7*
>
> *But every woman that prayeth or prophesieth with her head uncovered dishonoureth her head:*

for that is even all one as if she were shaven. ⁶For if the woman be not covered, let her also be shorn: but if it be a shame for a woman to be shorn or shaven, let her be covered. ⁷For a man indeed ought not to cover his head, forasmuch as he is the image and glory of God: but the woman is the glory of the man.

1 Corinthians 11:10
For this cause ought the woman to have power on her head because of the angels.

1 Corinthians 11:13
Judge in yourselves: is it comely that a woman pray unto God uncovered?

1 Corinthians 11:15
But if a woman have long hair, it is a glory to her: for her hair is given her for a covering.

We will get into the specifics of differentiation between a man and a woman with regard to hair. First, however, we must know that the connection between hair and submission to authority originates in the Old Testament.

In Numbers 5:11-31, we find what is called "the Law of Jealousies." Part of this law determined that when a woman's head was "uncovered," she lost her symbol of morality.

Some scholars believe that the sentence for those guilty of adultery was to have their heads shaved. This is based on the historical and grammatical application of the phrase "the woman shall be a curse among her people."

Another example of how hair was to show submission to authority is found in the law that addresses Jewish men marrying female prisoners of war (Deuteronomy 21:10-14). The very first thing he was to do when he got her home was to shave her head.

(This was because it was a mark of shame for a woman in ancient times.) Most scholars agree that once she became an Israelite, her hair would be allowed to grow again.

It is evident Paul was not simply "making up a rule" or dealing with some local custom. He was appealing to symbolism God had established centuries before the church came into existence.

These verses in 1 Corinthians 11 clearly state that the symbol of a man being in subjection to his authority is that his hair can never be long. The symbol of a woman's submission to her authority is that her hair MUST be long.

The question then arises, "How long is long?" We must examine the original Greek words used in 1 Corinthians 11:14-15 to find the answer.

> ***1 Corinthians 11:14-15***
> *Doth not even nature itself teach you, that, if a man have long hair, it is a shame unto him? [15]But if a woman have long hair, it is a glory to her: for her hair is given her for a covering.*

In these verses, the phrase "long hair" is actually just one word in Greek. That word is *komao*, which means "to let the hair grow."[104] Obviously, it is impossible to "let it grow" and cut it at the same time! This is clearly the intended meaning, based on what Paul had already said in verse 6.

> ***1 Corinthians 11:6***
> *For if the woman be not covered, let her also be shorn: but if it be a shame for a woman to be shorn or shaven, let her be covered.*

The word "shorn" is from the Greek word *keiro*, which

---

[104] Thayer, J., *A Greek-English Lexicon of the New Testament,* Baker Book House, 1993.

means "to shear; to cut off."[105] He goes on to say there is just as much "shame" associated with cutting the hair as with shaving it off altogether!

The real key to understanding how long "long" is comes from the opening phrase of verse 14. Paul appeals to nature as the determining factor. "Nature," he says, "teaches us."

Since the standard for a woman is to "let the hair grow," she should let nature decide "how long is long." She should do nothing to it chemically or manually that would in any way keep nature from determining the length of her hair. Once she uses a pair of scissors or applies any chemical or amount of heat that would in any way shorten her hair, nature is no longer in control.

Under this guideline, a woman whose hair simply won't grow beyond her shoulders is just as compliant as one whose hair reaches her ankles – so long as neither has interrupted the natural growth process! By the same token, a new convert may have extremely short hair when she is born again, but the moment her last haircut is covered by the blood, nature has once again been put in control. From that time forward, it can be considered "long" by Biblical standards.

Long hair is to be the visible symbol that the woman is under the "covering" of the authority in her life. As Paul said, "her hair is given her for a covering" (1 Corinthians 11:15).

Interestingly, the apostle said one reason a woman follows this practice is "because of the angels." What did he mean by that?

Angels serve many purposes, including being "ministering spirits" who serve the people of God. (See Hebrews 1:14.) We also see angels defending God's property, ready to judge any who

---

[105] Strong, James, *Strong's Exhaustive Concordance of the Bible,* Originally published 1890.

would violate His holiness. (See Genesis 3:24.)

It would seem, then, that the visible symbol of submission to authority provided by a woman's uncut hair is not only for the sake of humanity. She should have this "power" on her head "because of the angels" – they, too, need to see who is honoring God's holiness. In this way, they can properly determine whether to defend or judge the individual in question.

I will admit, however, that I cannot state this explanation with absolute confidence. It is conjecture on my part. Nevertheless, as explained in the previous paragraphs, it is based on my understanding of Scriptural principles.

Having established a Biblical standard for a woman's hair, we must now consider what is required of a man. Just as we did for the woman, we will look to Paul's appeal to nature to help us decide how "long" a man's hair should be.

A man is forbidden to have long hair, so he must keep it short. Furthermore, since a man's hair is NOT to grow beyond what nature teaches, it only makes sense that nature's guidelines must be followed. Accordingly, men have a "hairline" that is natural (*i.e.*, created by nature). That hairline goes above the ears, stays above the collar, and does not hang into the eyes. If a man will keep his hair cut to follow the natural hairline, he will never be accused of having "long" hair.

This standard of long hair on women and short hair on men can be confirmed in two ways. First, we appeal to the principle of gender distinction. This is based on Deuteronomy 22:5, which says, "The woman shall not wear that which pertaineth unto a man, neither shall a man put on a woman's garment: for all that do so are abomination unto the LORD thy God."

It is evident from this verse that God's original intent has been to maintain a clear distinction between the sexes. This applies not only to clothing but also to mannerisms (see 1

Corinthians 6:9). Therefore, we can use this same principle to teach a marked and easily recognizable distinction in the length of hair worn by each sex.

An interesting verse of Scripture in the Book of Revelation settles this issue. This verse proves that God intends for there to be a distinction between the length of a man's hair and that of a woman's.

> **Revelation 9:7-8**
> *And the shapes of the locusts were like unto horses prepared unto battle; and on their heads were as it were crowns like gold, and their faces were as the faces of men. ⁸And they had hair as the hair of women, and their teeth were as the teeth of lions.*

Please note that they had "the FACES of MEN." However, the writer went on to say they had "the HAIR of WOMEN." How else can this verse be explained except that God unquestionably expects a woman's hair to be distinctively different from a man's?

Second, we appeal to the principle of godly distinction. This is based on 2 Corinthians 6:17, which says, "Wherefore come out from among them, and be ye separate, saith the Lord, and touch not the unclean thing; and I will receive you."

In the same way that our clothing ought to proclaim a difference between saints and sinners, so should the length of our hair. We are to be separate from the world and should not base our hair length (or hairstyles, for that matter) on the ways of the ungodly.

I am well aware that much of the church world believes (and often asserts) that "Jesus had long hair." Their assertion is taken from paintings – NOT from Scripture! It is also worth noting that many of the artists who portrayed Jesus in such a manner were homosexual men living in the middle ages.

While some claim it was the custom of Jesus' day for men to wear their hair long, this is simply inaccurate. Drawings from that time period show men living in Israel during the time of Christ wearing their hair closely cropped.

An article on CNN's website provides some insight into this matter. In it, the author wrote, "[Richard] Neave and a team of researchers started with an Israeli skull dating back to the 1st century. They then used computer programs, clay, simulated skin and their knowledge about the Jewish people of the time to determine the shape of the face, and color of eyes and skin. They turned to the Bible to determine the length of his hair. In the New Testament, 'would Paul (one of the apostles) have written, "If a man has long hair, it is a disgrace to him" if Jesus Christ had had long hair?' the article speculates."[106]

The researchers correctly determined that Paul would not have called long hair on men a "disgrace" if Jesus Himself had long hair. After all, Paul had seen Jesus.

1 Corinthians 9:1
Am I not an apostle? am I not free? have I not seen Jesus Christ our Lord? are not ye my work in the Lord?

As the article points out, Paul would not condemn something practiced by His Lord? Obviously, Jesus did NOT have long hair!

Another argument commonly heard when trying to refute the hair-length distinctive is based on Paul's statement that "We have no such custom."

1 Corinthians 11:16
But if any man seem to be contentious, we have no such custom, neither the churches of God.

---

[106] Legon, Jeordan, CNN, *From Science and Computers, a New Face of Jesus*, https://www.cnn.com/2002/TECH/science/12/25/face.jesus/index.html

I don't want to come across as being rude towards those who espouse this idea, but I know of no other way to say it except, "This argument makes no sense!" It is unreasonable to believe Paul would spend time saying women must keep their hair long and men must keep theirs short only to come back and say, "If you don't like this, don't worry about it. Nobody else does it, either."

Commentator Adam Clark shed some light on what this verse actually says. He wrote, "If any person sets himself up as a ... defender of such points, that a woman may pray or teach with her head uncovered, and that a man may, without reproach, have long hair; let him know that we have no such custom as either, nor are they sanctioned by any of the Churches of God, whether among the Jews or the Gentiles."[107] In other words, Paul was saying we don't have a custom of women cutting their hair and men letting theirs grow long – not vice-versa!

As further proof, consider the *New Century Version*. It reads, "Some people may still want to argue about this, but I would add that neither we nor the churches of God have any other practice."[108]

We cannot conclude this chapter without addressing the issue of facial hair. I have heard many people (including some very conservative preachers) say there is no Bible for preaching against it except, "Obey them that have the rule over you" (Hebrews 13:17). I beg to differ.

Several Scriptural principles show why wearing facial hair is unacceptable. I will provide six examples.

- ***It is a symbol of uncleanness.***

The Jewish law required a man with leprosy to make himself readily recognizable to anyone who may come within viewing

---

[107] Clarke, Adam. *Adam Clarke's Commentary on the Bible*. Originally published 1810–1826.
[108] *The Holy Bible: New Century Version*, Thomas Nelson Publishers, 1991.

distance. This was accomplished not only by verbally announcing their uncleanness but also by manifesting a unique physical appearance.

> *Leviticus 13:45*
>
> *And the leper in whom the plague is, his clothes shall be rent, and his head bare, and he shall put a covering upon his upper lip, and shall cry, Unclean, unclean.*

He was instructed to "put a covering upon his upper lip." As I have already pointed out, the Apostle Paul applied the term "covering" to hair (see 1 Corinthians 11:4-15). Since this is the explanation given by a well-trained student of the Hebrew Scriptures, it is safe to infer that the law required the leper to wear a mustache!

This is not just my opinion. The *Jamieson-Fausset-Brown Commentary* makes a direct connection between the "covering upon his upper lip" mentioned in this verse and a mustache! It goes on to say that "the Hebrews used to shave the upper lip."[109]

God is the One Who established that covering the lip (with facial hair) is a symbol of uncleanness. Therefore, that principle will never change.

- **"Shamefacedness" Applies to Men.**

    1 Timothy 2:8-9

    I will therefore that men pray every where, lifting up holy hands, without wrath and doubting. ⁹In like manner also, that women adorn themselves in modest apparel, with shamefacedness and sobriety; not with broided hair, or gold, or pearls, or costly array;

---

[109] Jamieson, Robert, Andrew Robert Fausset, and David Brown, *Commentary on the Whole Bible*. Originally published 1871.

Hair: The Long and Short of It

In the last chapter, I explained the word "shamefaced" implies wearing nothing on one's face for the purpose of pride or flirtation. While this term is used when directly referring to women in verse 9, notice that the verse begins with the phrase, "In like manner also." Verse 8 was addressed to men, but this phrase ties the two verses together. Paul was saying to the women, "In the same way that men have to be holy, so must you." Therefore, whatever rules he established for the women would, by necessity, also apply to men.

If women cannot have anything on their faces because of pride or flirtation, then men must follow the same rule. Ask yourself if you have ever seen a man with facial hair who is not constantly "grooming," "stroking," or in some other manner bringing attention to it. I submit that, like a woman's makeup, facial hair on a man is almost certainly a matter of proving their "machismo" (which is pride) or an attempt to attract a partner (which is flirtation).

Even when people claim facial hair is part of their culture, they need to recognize being born again requires them to adopt the culture of God's Kingdom. When they say it's part of their ethnic identity, they are actually saying they are displaying ethnic pride.

- **Beards seem to be an "all or nothing" proposition in the Bible.**

There is no question that many Biblical characters wore beards. However, the wearing of beards came with distinct regulations.

> **Leviticus 19:27**
> *Ye shall not round the corners of your heads, neither shalt thou mar the corners of thy beard.*

> **Leviticus 21:5**
> *They shall not make baldness upon their head, neither shall they shave off the corner of their beard, nor make any cuttings in their flesh.*

These verses obviously do not prohibit the wearing of beards. However, they DO mandate that the beards be left untrimmed. If an Israelite was going to wear one, he had to let it grow without "marring" or "shaving off" the "corner of their beard." The *New Century Version* says, "You must not ... cut the edges of your beard."[110] *God's Word Translation* reads, "Never ... cut the edges of your beard."[111] Thus, if they were going to wear a beard, they had to let it grow without trimming it at all.

It seems highly improbable – if not impossible – to have any pride in an "unkempt" beard. Keeping it trimmed becomes a matter of pride and thus a violation of the principle of "shamefacedness."

- *We are Instructed to Hold to Good Traditions.*

  2 Thessalonians 2:15

  Therefore, brethren, stand fast, and hold the traditions which ye have been taught, whether by word, or our epistle.

Maintaining a clean-shaven appearance has been a tradition among the vast majority of apostolic men with whom I have been in fellowship. It has been this way for as long as I have been in the church. (I was born again in 1972.)

A survey was conducted a few years ago among the members of an Apostolic organization which showed that nearly 75% preferred to deal with those who wore no facial hair. Almost 80% said they believed wearing facial hair would have a negative impact on a man's ability to reach the lost.[112]

The same book reporting this survey also pointed out how many Charismatic leaders sport facial hair. The author suggested

---

[110] *The Holy Bible: New Century Version,* Thomas Nelson Publishers, 1991.
[111] *God's Word Translation,* Baker Books, 2010.
[112] Gore, Chancy, *Facial Hair - A Christian Perspective,* Advance Ministries, 1998.

that perhaps "free-growing hair is associated with free thinking and free living."[113]

- **We Should Not Be Associated with Wrong Crowds.**

    2 Corinthians 6:17
    Wherefore come out from among them, and be ye separate, saith the Lord, and touch not the unclean thing; and I will receive you,

The above-referenced volume went on to say, "Mainstream American society still links facial hair with a 60's lifestyle, long hair on men, rebellion, non-conformity and outright pride. The clean-shaven face serves the Christian well in avoiding these ills of society."[114]

The fact remains that many business owners and managers view facial hair as unprofessional and lacking in the clean image desired. Granted, not ALL feel this way, but many do.

As recently as a few years ago, studies showed that "people will have a more positive impression of a person's character if they don't have facial hair."[115] According to that study, only 3% of the population see a man with facial hair as being the most trustworthy.[116]

According to Allan Peterkin, a Toronto psychologist and professor, facial hair has always had negative connotations. In his book, Mr. Peterkin cites examples of "Good" men who were not clean-shaven: Santa Claus (obviously fictional), Jesus and the

---

[113] Gore, Chancy, *Facial Hair - A Christian Perspective,* Advance Ministries, 1998.
[114] *Ibid.*
[115] Cvetkovska, Ljubica, Modern Gentleman, *26 Beard Statistics and Facts You Probably Didn't Know,* https://moderngentlemen.net/beard-statistics
[116] *Ibid.*

disciples (which he cannot prove decisively). However, under the heading "The ... Bad," there is quite a list, including Attila the Hun, Blackbeard, Henry the VIII, Bluebeard, Ho Chi Minh, and Jesse James. Also, there was Ghengis Khan, Ivan the Terrible, Joseph Stalin, Adolph Hitler, Saddam Hussein, and Osama Bin Laden.[117]

However, the most troubling statistic concerning facial hair comes from the study mentioned earlier. It reports that homosexual men are more attracted to other men whose beards match their own.[118] That alone ought to cause any godly man to remain clean-shaven!

It is obviously much better to be associated with a godly crowd who has maintained a standard of not wearing facial hair than to have anyone think we may be part of any other group. I refuse even to take a chance of being identified with this ungodly world.

- **Some Things are Done for the Gospel's Sake.**
  Acts 15:24
  Forasmuch as we have heard, that certain which went out from us have troubled you with words, subverting your souls, saying, Ye must be circumcised, and keep the law: to whom we gave no such commandment:

In Acts 15, the issue of whether circumcision was essential for salvation was forever settled. Letters from the apostles were sent to all the churches, stating there was "no such commandment." The practice was not required and did not affect one's spiritual condition.

---

[117] Peterkin, Alan, *One Thousand Beards: A Cultural History of Facial Hair*, Arsenal Pulp Press, 2001.

[118] Cvetkovska, Ljubica, Modern Gentleman, *26 Beard Statistics and Facts You Probably Didn't Know*, https://moderngentlemen.net/beard-statistics

In spite of that decision, something noteworthy happened shortly thereafter. Paul circumcised Timothy.

Acts 16:1-3

Then came he to Derbe and Lystra: and, behold, a certain disciple was there, named Timotheus, the son of a certain woman, which was a Jewess, and believed; but his father was a Greek: ²Which was well reported of by the brethren that were at Lystra and Iconium. ³Him would Paul have to go forth with him; and took and circumcised him because of the Jews which were in those quarters: for they knew all that his father was a Greek.

Why would Paul insist Timothy do something that had just been declared unessential? According to Luke's account, it was "because of the Jews which were in those quarters." Even though it was not MANDATORY, Paul knew Timothy would be much better received by those he was trying to reach with the gospel. It may not have been necessary, but it WAS expedient so Timothy could be well-received among those he wanted to influence.

As I mentioned earlier, there is still a significant lack of trust in much of society for those who wear facial hair. Even if the Bible doesn't specifically say something is a sin, our desire to reach those around us should cause us to refrain from anything that might hamper our ability to gain their confidence.

Besides reaching the lost, there is another consideration when it comes to what is best for the furtherance of the gospel. Paul taught us to honor our brothers and sisters in the Lord by not doing anything that might offend them.

1 Corinthians 8:9-13

But take heed lest by any means this liberty of yours become a stumblingblock to them that are weak. ¹⁰*For if any man see thee which hast knowledge sit at meat in the idol's temple, shall not the conscience of him which is weak be emboldened to eat those things which are offered to idols;* ¹¹*And through thy knowledge shall the weak brother perish, for whom Christ died?* ¹²*But when ye sin so against the brethren, and wound their weak conscience, ye sin against Christ.* ¹³*Wherefore, if meat make my brother to offend, I will eat no flesh while the world standeth, lest I make my brother to offend.*

May God help each of us be willing to do whatever it may take to reach our world and keep from destroying our fellow saints. The reward will be well worth any sacrifice.

Hair: The Long and Short of It

PSALMS, HYMNS, AND SPIRITUAL SONGS

Ephesians 5:19
Speaking to yourselves in psalms and hymns and spiritual songs, singing and making melody in your heart to the Lord;

Colossians 3:16
Let the word of Christ dwell in you richly in all wisdom; teaching and admonishing one another in psalms and hymns and spiritual songs, singing with grace in your hearts to the Lord.

There is a vast difference between church music and music in the church. Not all music heard in churches today can be rightly termed acceptable "church music."

On two separate occasions, writing to two different churches, the Apostle Paul specified the kinds of music that are acceptable. In both Ephesians 5:19 and Colossians 3:16, he listed the exact same three categories of musical style. Under the inspiration of the Holy Ghost, he said to use "psalms and hymns and spiritual songs." No other forms of music are ever identified by him – or any other New Testament author – as being permissible.

The word "psalms," of course, deals with the Old Testament songs by that name or other songs which would fit into that category. They are songs of inspiration and hope, written to be used with instrumental accompaniment. They should be full of praise and have the sole purpose of either entreating God or giving glory to Him – or both. They should inspire worship within the hearts of the singer as well as the hearer.

Strong's Exhaustive Concordance defines the word "hymn" in these verses as "a religious ode."[119] The word "ode" is defined as literature written in an "elaborate ... form and expressive of exalted ... emotion."[120] Hymns are songs of praise or sacred songs. These include the traditional hymns of the church that possess a style of music that is majestic and beautiful. They are harmonious and flowing. They speak of foundational truths and frequently invite the sinner to be saved.

The third type of music to be used is "spiritual songs." Notice the adjective "spiritual." It was inserted by Paul for a reason. The word "songs" comes from a generic Greek word and might be used of songs that are anything BUT spiritual. It is a general word for a song, whether of praise or any other subject. Hence, adding the descriptive term "spiritual" is necessary.

The word "spiritual" is translated from a Greek word meaning "that which is opposed to the carnal." It appeals to the heart and soul as distinguished from the flesh. Thus, the songs we sing – or listen to – should never appeal primarily to the flesh.

Since the Biblically approved styles of music must be either psalms, hymns, or spiritual songs, we need to know how to recognize these types of music. Doing so will help us differentiate between "music in the church" and proper "church music."

It is impossible to make this distinction without knowing some basic facts about music in general. Most importantly, you should know all music consists of three parts: melody, harmony,

---

[119] Strong, James, *Strong's Exhaustive Concordance of the Bible*, Originally published 1890.

[120] Dictionary.com, www.dictionary.com

and rhythm.

Before delving into those three parts, there is something else we should consider. When God created humanity, He created US with three parts.

> ***1 Thessalonians 5:23***
> *And the very God of peace sanctify you wholly; and I pray God your whole spirit and soul and body be preserved blameless unto the coming of our Lord Jesus Christ.*

Man consists of spirit, soul, and body. Each of these fills a unique role in our lives.

The term "body" is self-explanatory. It is our fleshly "tabernacle" which houses our spirit and our soul.

There is much debate among scholars when it comes to explaining the latter terms. According to Thayer's Greek Lexicon, the spirit is "the rational part of man, the power of perceiving and grasping divine and eternal things."[121] The soul is defined as "the breath of life; the vital force which animates the body."[122]

I will not take the time to express my opinions on this matter. The only point I want to make is that one is more superficial than the other.

It seems apparent that these three parts could be said to be "levels" within man. Our fleshly desires, our human intellect and emotions, and the longing within us for divine connection all have an impact on us in varying degrees.

Thus, both man and music have three distinct components. Interestingly, each component of man is directly affected by a particular component of music.

---

[121] Thayer, J., *A Greek-English Lexicon of the New Testament,* Baker Book House, 1993.
[122] *Ibid.*

Melody is the fundamental part of music. It is designed to take the lead. In proper musical formats, it will always be the most prominent aspect of any song. For those who are not musically inclined, the melody is what a soloist sings. It is what we call the "tune" of the song.

Harmony is the arrangement of chords added to support the melody. It should do just that – *support*. If you ever hear someone sing lines meant to harmonize without having someone sing the melody, it sounds awkward and unusual.

To help explain this for those with no musical knowledge, imagine someone at a piano playing a song with just one finger. That is the melody. When the pianist adds both hands, however, he or she is adding the notes of harmony. It creates a fuller, richer sound as the other notes blend with the "one-finger" notes.

Rhythm, of course, is the beat. It should never lead but should always be the accompaniment for the melody and harmony. Its purpose should be to keep the other parts in time with each other.

Because the melody is the most fundamental aspect of any piece of music, it appeals to the most superficial part of man. Adding harmony causes the music to reach deeper into the individual, creating a level of fulness the melody cannot accomplish on its own.

The rhythm has a direct appeal to the flesh. How often have you caught yourself tapping your foot or moving your body to some song, not even realizing you had begun to do so? There is a reason why this happens!

Our body depends on rhythm. If we are healthy, our hearts beat at regular intervals. Our lungs expand and contract with rhythmic breathing. Nearly everything about us as human beings is dependent on timing in one way or another.

The problem is that rhythm appeals to the flesh more intensely than most of us realize. It can become a driving force, sometimes causing a regrettable response.

Not everything that appeals to the flesh is necessarily wrong, of course. (One example is food.) However, ANYTHING that appeals to fleshly appetites MUST be controlled. Whenever things appealing to flesh are given the primary role and purpose, they ALWAYS lead to spiritual destruction.

So it is in the case of music. As long as it remains in its proper place, rhythm is a great tool that holds a song together. On the other hand, if rhythm becomes the focal point in music, it creates a very carnal response. In those cases, regardless of the lyrics, the music does not lead us to a place of spirituality. It inevitably does just the opposite.

Never underestimate the power of music. Restaurant owners have learned to use "piped-in" music to control their customers' speed of selecting entrees and eating. They know music with a fast pace will cause "rush hour" customers to hurry through the lines, eat quickly, and thereby make room for others. They also know slower music can be used when there are no crowds, assuring that customers will take their time going through the lines and probably purchase more as a result.

The reason for this is physiological. As you listen to a piece of music, even though you are unaware of it, your entire body is constantly reacting to the sounds it hears. Variations in pitch, rhythmic patterns, tempo, and volume will affect your pulse rate, blood pressure, respiration, and the function of certain glands, creating a mood or eliciting a physical action. All of this comes as an automatic, subconscious response over which you have no control.

Music has a powerful effect on us. Like the human body, it consists of many "tension/resolution" situations.

When you are hungry, you eat and resolve your hunger. If you are thirsty, you can quench your thirst with a cool drink. Feeling hot? Find some shade. Whenever you are tired, you can get some rest. These tensions all require resolution.

Psalms, Hymns, and Spiritual Songs

Furthermore, tension may be experienced by proxy. If you listen to a speaker with a "frog in his throat," you will begin trying to clear yours. If you hear a singer hang on and on to his final note, you most likely will start gasping for air.

Moreover, different musical sounds will affect different parts of the body. A high pitch will cause the larynx to tighten. A fast rhythm will set the foot to tapping. This is the tension release factor.

Music is built upon this factor. It is made up of chords which produce tension. Normally, those chords will be followed by chords that resolve that tension. The fewer tensions in the music, the more calming effect it will have on the listener. (This is one of the main principles behind using music for therapy.) Some music, however, is full of tension with no resolution. This builds physical and emotional frustration within the hearer. When not resolved musically, this frustration generally finds its resolution in negative behavior.

If you know someone who plays a keyboard, ask them to play a "suspended chord." Have them hit the same chord repeatedly for several seconds. Doing so will leave everyone within earshot feeling frustrated until that "sus" chord (as it's called) is resolved.

Without getting too technical, let me explain. A suspended chord replaces the third (the note defining whether a chord is major or minor) with either a second or a fourth, creating a floaty, unresolved sound. It's like hitting pause on the harmony because tension hangs in the air, begging to resolve back to a standard chord. Think of it as a musical cliffhanger.

Take a C major chord: C (root), E (third), G (fifth). The E makes it major. Swap that E for a D (the second note in the C scale), and you get C-D-G – called a "Csus2." If you swap E for an F (the fourth), making it a C-F-G, it is called a "Csus4." Neither has a third, so it's neither major nor minor—just suspended, waiting. The "sus" label comes from a medieval musical practice, where a note was "suspended" from a previous chord and then resolved. Today, it has become a static sound.

One could say that a sus chord is like the human spirit: ever reaching. However, it remains unsettled. The resolved chord would be more like the soul: grounded.

This process of building tension and resolving it explains why some music can make you relax and bring feelings of peace and contentment. Music with little or no resolution causes frustration, nervousness, or even depression.

Because it is such an influential tool, music serves an important purpose. It can bring about powerful results when used properly and devastating ones when used improperly.

The Bible tells of a time when the prophet Elisha was obviously frustrated with some of his audience but recognized his need to hear from God. At that point, he made a request he knew would help him "get in the Spirit."

> *2 Kings 3:14-15*
>
> *And Elisha said, As the LORD of hosts liveth, before whom I stand, surely, were it not that I regard the presence of Jehoshaphat the king of Judah, I would not look toward thee, nor see thee. [15]But now bring me a minstrel. And it came to pass, when the minstrel played, that the hand of the LORD came upon him.*

In this instance, music helped the man of God reach a place where he could better surrender himself to the Spirit. As a result, he was used of God.

Before becoming king, David was called upon to deal with an evil spirit tormenting Saul. He did it by playing music, which evidently drove away the demon.

> *1 Samuel 16:23*
>
> *And it came to pass, when the evil spirit from*

> God was upon Saul, that David took an harp, and played with his hand: so Saul was refreshed, and was well, and the evil spirit departed from him.

Seeing the effect good music can have in driving away evil spirits, it stands to reason that the WRONG music can INVITE them. After more than 40 years of studying the effects of music,[123] I have come to the conclusion it not only CAN attract demonic influences, but in many cases, it absolutely DOES!

It is not a coincidence music was involved during Israel's worship of the golden calf. While Moses recognized it as the "noise of them that sing" (Exodus 32:18), to Joshua, it sounded like the "noise of war" (Exodus 32:17). While it cannot be proven conclusively that the music was the reason, it is undeniable that SOMETHING compelled the people to strip off their clothes and dance around the idol.

When Nebuchadnezzar wanted to get people to bow before the image he had built, music was once again involved. (See Daniel 3:5.) This music must have mesmerized the people into worshipping an idol since he intended to have the musicians start playing again for the three Hebrews who refused to bow. (See Daniel 3:15.)

In spite of this, many people still try to excuse their use of ungodly forms of music. They often claim they are only trying to reach younger people or appeal to a wider audience. I will not question the validity of their motives. I will only say having the right motive while using the wrong method does not negate the action's negative impact. It does not spare those involved from the negative consequences, either.

Some years after he assumed the throne, King David decided to bring the Ark of the Covenant to Jerusalem. To accomplish this

---

[123] My first book was entitled *The Madness and Method of Modern Music* and was originally published in 1988.

goal, he "carried the ark of God in a new cart" (1 Chronicles 13:7). This was in direct opposition to the command of God. The Lord had ordered that the ark was to be carried upon the shoulders of the Levites, specifically the sons of Kohath. (See Exodus 25:10-15 and Numbers 3:30-31; 4:4, 15)

David's procession was a mighty display of joy and reverence, yet it resulted in tragedy. As the oxen pulling the cart hit a rough spot in the road, the ark began to shake. Uzzah, one of those helping with the procession, tried to "help God out" by putting "forth his hand to the ark of God, and took hold of it" (II Samuel 6:6).

Again, this was against God's command. In Numbers 4:15, we read, "They shall not touch any holy thing, lest they die." Accordingly, "the anger of the Lord was kindled against Uzzah, and he smote him" (I Chronicles 13:10).

Uzzah did not die because the Lord was opposed to the return of the ark. If David had followed God's command to allow the priests to carry the ark, the rough road would never have affected the procession.

God was not even opposed to the motives involved. Instead, He was opposed to the method. Even though David was doing the right thing with the right motive, he was doing it in the wrong way. As a result, God was sorely displeased.

Stories that confirm this principle are plenteous throughout the Scripture. For example, consider the example of Cain and Abel and their respective offerings.

Abel, "a keeper of sheep" (Genesis 4:2), brought to the Lord "of the firstlings of his flock and of the fat thereof. And the LORD had respect unto Abel and his offering" (Genesis 4:4). Cain, however, as a "tiller of the ground...brought of the fruit of the ground" (Genesis 4:2-3). Cain's sacrifice was rejected as sin (see Genesis 4:7). This rejection was not because of his motive but because of his method.

Using carnal, worldly methods can never produce spiritual, godly results! We cannot sanctify sin! Furthermore, we must recognize that this is just as true of the subject of music as it is of any other topic.

We should no longer hide under the guise of "pure motives." While a person may be sincere, it is possible to be sincerely wrong. The motive behind our music may be entirely pure, but if our method is wrong, we should be aware of God's ultimate disapproval. Don't forget how the Lord rebuked Israel for offering "polluted bread" upon His altar.

Malachi 1:7
Ye offer polluted bread upon mine altar; and ye say, Wherein have we polluted thee? In that ye say, The table of the LORD *is contemptible.*

God is not obligated to conform to our tastes. Rather, we have an obligation to conform to His will. If our preferences are contrary to God's approval, we must be willing to submit to Him. If we are going to call Him Lord, we must permit Him to be Lord (the One Who reigns sovereign) over our life, our desires, our will—and our music!

John 14:15
If ye love me, keep my commandments.

When it comes to music that is considered unacceptable, we must realize this is not about personal preferences. I'm not talking about "new songs" versus "old songs." The age of the song has no impact on whether it is godly or ungodly.

Numerous Scriptures actually instruct us to "sing a new song," such as Psalm 33:3, 96:1, 98:1, 149:1, and many more. In fact, I'll go so far as to say if someone has a problem with singing "new songs," they should not plan to go to Heaven because singing a "new song" is something John witnessed happening on more than one occasion (see Revelation 5:9 and 14:3).

What is being dealt with here is music that is carnal in its nature – not only in the lyrics but in the music itself. As I explained earlier, if the most prominent feature of the music is the rhythm, it appeals mainly to the flesh. Therefore, it cannot rightfully be considered a "spiritual song."

Ungodly music was not born in modern times! It didn't arrive on our shores from a foreign continent. It didn't start in nightclubs, honky-tonks, barrooms, or rock concerts.

The kind of music I'm writing about began before creation. It originated in the heart of Lucifer. Please allow me to offer proof.

Some scholars believe Lucifer was the first "worship leader." For one thing, the name "Lucifer" in the original Hebrew is *heylel* (pronounced "hey-leel"). It comes from the word *halal*, which is the root of our word "hallelujah."

Halal means "to shine, to praise, to boast, to be clamorously foolish." The suffix "jah" directs this "to Jehovah." Thus, "hallelujah" literally means to "praise Jehovah."

In many places in the Psalms (like Psalm 150), we read, "Praise ye the Lord." The Hebrew actually says, "Hallelujah!"

As you can see, Lucifer's name is connected to the word for the most intense worship of God. This is why many people believe he was Heaven's worship leader.

There is a second reason as well. Music was created in him.

Ezekiel 28:13-14

Thou hast been in Eden the garden of God; every precious stone was thy covering, the sardius, topaz, and the diamond, the beryl, the onyx, and the jasper, the sapphire, the emerald, and the carbuncle, and gold: the workmanship of thy tabrets and of thy pipes was prepared in thee in the day that thou wast created. [14]Thou art the anointed cherub that covereth; and I have set thee so: thou wast upon the holy mountain of God; thou hast walked up and down in the midst of the stones of fire.

If, in fact, Lucifer WAS the original worship leader, what happened to him? How did he end up so far from his original purpose? Isaiah provides the answers to these questions.

Isaiah 14:12-15
How art thou fallen from heaven, O Lucifer, son of the morning! how art thou cut down to the ground, which didst weaken the nations! [13]For thou hast said in thine heart, I will ascend into heaven, I will exalt my throne above the stars of God: I will sit also upon the mount of the congregation, in the sides of the north: [14]I will ascend above the heights of the clouds; I will be like the most High. [15]Yet thou shalt be brought down to hell, to the sides of the pit.

At some point along the way, the one who was supposed to be boasting about God began boasting about himself! Rather than seeking to give God glory, he started seeking glory for himself! Lucifer quit exalting God and started seeking and expecting attention for himself.

This change in focus resulted in a change in character. In the end, it cost him his position.

Ezekiel 28:15
Thou wast perfect in thy ways from the day that thou wast created, till iniquity was found in thee.

When he stopped praising God, evil began to spring up in him. Eventually, Lucifer's pride resulted in the ultimate act of rebellion! He was cast out of Heaven, taking one-third of the angels with him. (See Revelation 12:4.)

As was stated earlier, Ezekiel 28:13 says, "The workmanship

of thy tabrets and of thy pipes was prepared in thee in the day that thou wast created." Therefore, we know the devil was created with music in him. Is it unreasonable to suppose that everything within him—including his music—was broken when he was cast to the ground (Ezekiel 28:17)? If so, it would further stand to reason that the "broken" music within him is still being used to lead people astray!

Even though God created music, that does not mean that every variation and type please Him. The enemy loves to take what God creates and pervert its purpose.

Just because He created music does NOT mean He has no boundaries on its usage (ESPECIALLY when it comes to worship)! As with most of His creation, God typically provides certain parameters to govern its usage.

I contend that Lucifer (in whom some form of music was created) has twisted the purpose (and, in some cases, the style) of music that was intended for the worship of Jehovah. Instead, he uses it for self-gratification and self-glorification. In the process, he gets man to use it for the same self-serving purposes!

Make no mistake — it was when Lucifer ceased uplifting God and put the focus on himself that he was cast out of Heaven and, consequently, became Satan. I submit that the minute our music is more focused on the musician and/or singer and/or "dancer" than the One Who is SUPPOSED to be the focus, that music is no longer "heavenly," regardless of WHERE it was created. There is simply no room for magnifying the flesh while trying to entertain God's Spirit.

1 Corinthians 1:29
That no flesh should glory in his presence.

While I'm addressing the danger of using music that glorifies the flesh, I want to address what seems to be a trend in some Apostolic churches. It is concerning, to say the least.

In my opinion, too many churches are putting on productions that bring attention to the individuals rather than leading people into the presence of God. The choreographed steps and hand gestures may cause the crowd to be awed by the performers, but it is doubtful these actions are moving anyone to true depths of worship.

What is the purpose behind these orchestrated movements? I cannot imagine they are being done because the participants think God enjoys it. Yet EVERYTHING was created (and should be used) for God's pleasure – NOT ours. That includes music!

> **Revelation 4:11**
> *Thou art worthy, O Lord, to receive glory and honour and power: for thou hast created all things, and for thy pleasure they are and were created.*

If a song is filled with unresolved tension, emphasizes the beat above the melody and harmony, and/or brings glory to anyone but the Lord, it should never be sung or played in His house. There can be no union of good and evil. It is simply not possible to mix the Spirit of a holy God with music designed by the unholy enemy of our soul.

> **2 Corinthians 6:14-15**
> *Be ye not unequally yoked together with unbelievers: for what fellowship hath righteousness with unrighteousness? and what communion hath light with darkness? [15]And what concord hath Christ with Belial? or what part hath he that believeth with an infidel?*

Paul said the use of things given to devils is fellowshipping with devils. It is not beyond the pale, then, to consider music which came from devils even worse!

I Corinthians 10:20
But I say, that the things which the Gentiles sacrifice, they sacrifice to devils, and not to God: and I would not that ye should have fellowship with devils.

I want to be clear in helping you recognize musical styles that would be displeasing to God. The most notable factor about such music is, of course, the overpowering beat.

Much of today's music stresses the beat over any other part of the song. This is because rhythm appeals to the flesh. What do you hear when a teen passes you in his car with the music blaring? More than anything else, you will always recognize the rhythm. Its major emphasis is on the rhythm rather than the melody. It has a driving, "broken" form about it.

When it comes to rap, there IS no melody or harmony. It is ONLY rhythm. It is fleshly and carnal. There is no redeeming value, regardless of the lyrics.

The second characteristic of an unacceptable song is the extensive use of "syncopation." By this, I mean a disturbance or interruption of the regular flow of rhythm. To put it simply, syncopation is the accenting of any normally unaccented beat. In other words, rather than accenting the "on-beat" or the "off-beat," syncopation is rhythmically "in the cracks."

Third, beware of any music that employs excessive volume. It is reported that the average decibels of a rock concert is between 90 and 100, with some concerts registering more than 130 decibels![124]

"An over 14-minute exposure to decibel levels above 100 dB can cause hearing damage. ... Depending on how high the decibel level is, even a short-time exposure can be damaging. For

---

[124] Decibel Pro, *Rock Concert Decibels Estimated,* https://decibelpro.app/blog/how-loud-is-a-rock-concert,

instance, an over 2-hour exposure to decibel levels above 90 dB can lead to hearing damage. In the same way, an over 2-minute exposure to decibel levels above 110 dB can lead to hearing damage/loss."[125]

The damage, however, doesn't stop at your ears. "Prolonged exposure to loud music can actually alter the structure of your brain. It's like repeatedly hitting a drum – eventually, you're going to leave a dent. These alterations can affect how your brain processes sound and may even impact cognitive functions beyond hearing."[126]

A final "tell-tale" sign a song can be classified as unacceptable is the musical tension I mentioned earlier. Much of today's music is full of tension, with little (or no) resolution. It is anything but relaxing. It is definitely not conducive to worship (except, perhaps, in the case of worshipping idols).

Ungodly music is filled with musical tension without resolution. The frustration that is created can – and often does – result in the most extremely negative behavior imaginable. This is no doubt an important factor in the increase in violence and pregnancy among teens.

A physicist and a neurobiologist once conducted an experiment to test the effects of background sounds on laboratory mice. Harvey Bird of Fairleigh Dickinson University in Rutherford, New Jersey, and Gervasia Schreckenberg of Georgian Court College in Lakewood, New Jersey, had one group of mice spend eight weeks exposed to the discordant drumbeat of rock. According to Schreckenberg, when placed in a maze, these mice took much longer to find their food. They were wandering off with

---

[125] Decibel Pro, *Rock Concert Decibels Estimated*, https://decibelpro.app/blog/how-loud-is-a-rock-concert

[126] NeuroLaunch, *Music's Negative Effects on the Brain: Exploring the Dark Side of Melodies*, https://neurolaunch.com/how-music-affects-the-brain-negatively

no sense of direction. The mice that had spent eight weeks listening to Johan Strauss waltzes performed normally. When dissected, the brains of the rats that had been subjected to eight weeks of rock music revealed abnormal neuron structures in the region associated with learning memory."[127]

If we understand the dangers of this style of music, we will cease to allow our young people – or ourselves – to feed on such a destructive influence. As we showed in chapter 7, the Bible instructs us not to defile or harm the temple of our body.

1 Corinthians 3:17
If any man defile the temple of God, him shall God destroy; for the temple of God is holy, which temple ye are.

1 Corinthians 6:19
What? know ye not that your body is the temple of the Holy Ghost which is in you, which ye have of God, and ye are not your own?

"Defiling" or harming the temple of your body can be done in more ways than adultery, tobacco, and alcohol. If certain types of music really do destroy the nerve cells of our brains and damage our hearing, those styles should be avoided at all costs!

To this point, I have not even addressed the lyrics. Although this chapter is dedicated to "Christian" music (as opposed to secular music), I should at least mention that the words of most secular songs (including "Country Music") are so ungodly they certainly do not fit into the category of "psalms, hymns, and spiritual songs." Secular songs are generally vile and anti-biblical in their content. Regardless of whether we might be able to classify the STYLE of music as wrong, if the LYRICS are

---

[127] Schreckenberg, G. M., & Bird, H. H. *Neural Plasticity of Mus Musculus in Response to Disharmonic Sound.* The Bulletin of the New Jersey Academy of Science. 1987.

detestable, no child of God should willingly choose to listen to it.

Philippians 4:8
Finally, brethren, whatsoever things are true, whatsoever things are honest, whatsoever things are just, whatsoever things are pure, whatsoever things are lovely, whatsoever things are of good report; if there be any virtue, and if there be any praise, think on these things.

Even if a song has Christian lyrics, that does not necessarily make it a "good" song. Many of today's contemporary songs are full of tension with no resolution. It is difficult to get into a deep spirit of true worship while listening. It can drive a congregation into an emotional frenzy, but that is not worship. Sadly enough, however, this sound has all but replaced the hymns and gospel songs that once were sung as an expression of worship and praise. Those songs brought comfort and inspiration to countless church members. Not so today.

Once again, I want to emphatically state that I am not saying all "new songs" are wrong. I am simply trying to help you realize you can't just "accept" anything and everything that comes down the pike under the guise of "Christian music."

Many of today's songs are little more than musical junk food with absolutely no spiritual nutrition. The "7-11" choruses (using the same seven words sung eleven times) are flooding our churches.

I have some serious concerns when people say we need to adopt the world's musical styles to reach the lost. First, nowhere does God say He intends for music to be a method of salvation. He chose the "foolishness of preaching," not foolish singing (I Corinthians 1:21)!

1 Corinthians 1:21
For after that in the wisdom of God the world by wisdom knew not God, it pleased God by the

> *foolishness of preaching to save them that believe.*

Secondly, I am convinced that if today's youth is "turned off," it is not because of music. If anything has turned them off, it has been the hypocrisy of much of the older generation. Most young people today simply will not be fooled by a religious mask. They are looking for something BETTER than what they possess – something that will change them. They are not looking for the same thing they have, just in a different suit!

I highly recommend everyone approach with skepticism any "contemporary" treatment of religious subjects. If there is a message at all, it is most likely not the kind of message we really want our young people to be getting.

Whether or not we want to admit it, "Contemporary Christian Music" is a money-making project. The artists are, for the most part, capitalizing on the name of Christ. Who can count the number of secular musicians who, upon hitting the bottom of their charts, suddenly were "saved." Their "salvation," however, only seemed to last long enough to get them financially on their feet again. Then, all too often, they were gone, taking many followers with them.

In her book, *God Gave Rock & Roll to You*, author Leah Payne described many of today's "mega-churches." She wrote that they "learned how to grow big churches with elaborate rock-concert-style worship experiences."[128] This sounds very much like what I'm seeing in some Apostolic churches today. They are painting the sanctuary black, using strobe lights and fog machines, and filling the platform with multi-colored LED lights and "background" scenes. They are turning up the volume and providing the crowds with a "top-notch" production.

---

[128] Payne, Leah, *God Gave Rock & Roll to You: a history of contemporary Christian music,* Oxford University Press, 2024.

Unfortunately, using a method birthed by the charismatic movement will most likely result in the gradual transformation from an Apostolic church into a charismatic assembly.

By the way, there is no such thing as "Christian Rock" or "Christian Rap." If it is rock or rap, it is not Christian. If it is Christian, it is definitely not rock or rap. Saying "Christian Rock" is like saying "Christian Cigarettes" or "Christian Alcohol" or "Christian Fornication." There is simply no way to put the two together. There is nothing Christian about either style of music. You simply cannot have both. To try and do so is much like the attitude of the Israelites, who "feared the Lord and served their own gods" (II Kings 17:33).

> *2 Kings 17:33*
> *They feared the LORD, and served their own gods, after the manner of the nations whom they carried away from thence.*

In my opening remarks, I pointed out how the Apostle Paul specifically told us what kinds of music we are permitted to use: "psalms and hymns and spiritual songs." No other forms of music are ever referred to as being permissible.

Therefore, the songs we sing should be psalms, hymns, or spiritual songs. As I have already explained, the word "spiritual" simply means, "that which is opposed to the carnal." It pertains to the heart and soul as distinguished from the flesh. Thus, the songs we sing – or listen to – should never appeal to the flesh.

Romans instructs us, "But put ye on the Lord Jesus Christ, and make not provision for the flesh to fulfill the lusts thereof" (Romans 13:14). OUR MUSIC SHOULD NEVER APPEAL PRIMARILY TO OUR FLESH! If it does, it cannot be classified as a "spiritual song."

I wholeheartedly believe it is high time we awaken ourselves to what is happening. It is time that every one of us take a stand against what could be called "Satan's Trojan Horse" – ungodly music being accepted by a once holy people.

If a person were to survey the young people who listen to much of today's more contemporary "Christian" music, it is highly probable they would find that most of them are addicted to the music and don't care where it comes from. They have no problem, therefore, when it comes to "crossing over" from "Contemporary Christian" to secular songs that sound much the same. Unfortunately, many of them are already there.

My concerns are summed up in the words of Dr. Albert Barnes, who wrote about the music of the New Testament Church. He said, "Their psalms and hymns were to be regarded as a method of teaching and admonishing; that is, they were to be imbued with truth, and to be such as to elevate the mind, and withdraw it from error and sin. Dr. Johnson once said that if he were allowed to make the ballads of a nation, he cared not who made the laws. It is true in a more important sense that he who is permitted to make the hymns of a church need care little who preaches or who makes the creed. He will more effectually mold the sentiments of a church than they who preach or make creeds and confessions. Hence, it is indispensable, in order to [ensure] the preservation of the truth that the sacred songs of a church should be imbued with sound evangelical sentiment."[129]

Parents, we must not accept the devil's deceitful terms of leaving our children in his deadly grasp (see Exodus 10:10-11). Young people, don't fall into Satan's trap of accepting music wrapped in "Christian" lyrics. Instead, let us wholeheartedly take a stand against the madness and the method of ungodly music.

---

[129] Barnes, A., J. G. Murphy, F. C. Cook, E. B. Pusey, H.C. Leupold, & R. Frew, Barnes' Notes. Blackie & Son, 1847.

GRIEVE NOT THE SPIRIT

Ephesians 4:30
And grieve not the holy Spirit of God, whereby ye are sealed unto the day of redemption.

Perhaps one of the most significant challenges with writing a book on holiness and separation is that some people may expect it to be exhaustive. By this, I mean they think it will be all-inclusive, dealing with every possible issue – and, therefore, if something is NOT addressed, it must be acceptable (or, at the least, not important enough to address). It is also possible that, as the author, I may be accused of not wanting to take a stand on a particular issue. However, such thinking is simplistic at best.

It would be impossible for anyone to cover every topic related to issues of separation in one book. For one thing, the world is constantly changing – new problems and temptations are going to arise, possibly causing any such attempt to become outdated.

Furthermore, such a vast array of carnal appeals already exists that it would be logistically impossible to deal with them all. An undertaking of that magnitude would require many volumes!

In this final chapter, I want to touch on a few principles encompassing most of what I have not yet covered. I will offer principles to help with the proper method of addressing new worldly advances unknown at the time of this writing.

Early in this exposition, I dealt with the importance of having a "right spirit." (If necessary, you might want to go back and reread that chapter before continuing.) Nevertheless, there is an aspect of maintaining a right spirit upon which I feel needs to be expounded.

In Ephesians 4, the Apostle Paul wrote about things requiring our focus. He seems to put special emphasis on the things our spirit manifests.

> ***Ephesians 4:22-29***
> *That ye put off concerning the former conversation the old man, which is corrupt according to the deceitful lusts; ^{23}And be renewed in the spirit of your mind; ^{24}And that ye put on the new man, which after God is created in righteousness and true holiness. ^{25}Wherefore putting away lying, speak every man truth with his neighbour: for we are members one of another. ^{26}Be ye angry, and sin not: let not the sun go down upon your wrath: ^{27}Neither give place to the devil. ^{28}Let him that stole steal no more: but rather let him labour, working with his hands the thing which is good, that he may have to give to him that needeth. ^{29}Let no corrupt communication proceed out of your mouth, but that which is good to the use of edifying, that it may minister grace unto the hearers.*

In verse 22, he says to "put off the former lifestyle." In verse 23, he instructs us to be "renewed" in our spirit. Verse 24 tells us to put on a new and holy man. Verse 25 commands us to quit lying. In verse 26, we read that we should control our temper. Verse 27 informs us we must not make room for temptation. Verse 28 basically orders men to quit stealing and get to work. In verse 29, the apostle reminds us to be careful what we say. Everything mentioned involves always keeping a right spirit.

He didn't stop there. Not only must we guard our spirit, however. We must also strive to never "grieve" God's Spirit.

Ephesians 4:30
And grieve not the holy Spirit of God, whereby ye are sealed unto the day of redemption.

This was an important appeal to the church at Ephesus when he told them (and, by extension, every Christian) not to grieve God's Spirit. The significance of what was being said could easily go unnoticed without taking the time to dig deeper into its meaning.

The Greek word translated "grieve" in this passage is used in a number of other ways throughout the New Testament. In every case, however, the translation shows sorrow or sadness. For example, it is rendered "sorrowful" (Matthew 14:9, 17:23, 18:31, 19:22, 26:22, 26:37; Mark 14:19; John 16:20; 2 Corinthians 2:2, 6:10, 7:8-9, 11; 1 Thessalonians 4:13), "grieve" or "grieved" (Mark 10:22; John 21:17; Romans 14:15; 2 Corinthians 2:4-5; Ephesians 4:30), and "in heaviness" (1 Peter 1:6).

How could it be possible for mortal man to make the Spirit of God "sorrowful," "grieved," or "in heaviness?" Does the Spirit of God feel sadness as a result of the actions of men? He absolutely does!

This should not seem to be such a far stretch for our minds to comprehend inasmuch as we know certain actions have definitely moved God to anger. If He can experience anger, why would we be surprised that He would also experience sadness?

In the very first book of the Bible, we see that God does, indeed, feel grief. According to the Book of Genesis, the wickedness of mankind moved God to grieve.

Genesis 6:5-6

And GOD saw that the wickedness of man was great in the earth, and that every imagination of the thoughts of his heart was only evil continually. ⁶And it repented the LORD that he had made man on the earth, and it grieved him at his heart.

Concerning this passage, Matthew Henry writes, "Here is ... God's resentment of man's wickedness. He did not see it as an unconcerned spectator, but as one injured and affronted by it; he saw it as a tender father sees the folly and stubbornness of a rebellious and disobedient child, which not only angers him, but grieves him, and makes him wish he had been ... childless."[130]

Sin and ungodliness grieve God! Other passages confirm this by also describing how the sinfulness of mankind affects God.

Amos 2:13

Behold, I am pressed under you, as a cart is pressed that is full of sheaves.

Here, the word "pressed" means "weighed down, to be crushed. It is used of a heavy weight pressing down on something. In context, it is used figuratively to show the weight of Israel's rebelliousness in pressing down on God."[131] Sin breaks His heart!

Isaiah 43:24

Thou hast bought me no sweet cane with money, neither hast thou filled me with the fat of thy sacrifices: but thou hast made me to serve with thy sins, thou hast wearied me with thine iniquities.

---

[130] Henry, M., *Matthew Henry's Commentary on the Whole Bible,* Fleming H. Revell, 1935.
[131] Baker, W., & E. E. Carpenter, *The Complete Word Study Dictionary: Old Testament,* AMG Publishers. 2003.

In this verse, the Lord said He was "wearied" with their iniquities. Their spiritual wickedness caused God to be "grieved." The Book of Psalms also uses this same word ("grieved").

Psalms 95:10
Forty years long was I grieved with this generation, and said, It is a people that do err in their heart, and they have not known my ways:

The Hebrew word used here literally means "to loathe, to nauseate, to be disgusted with."[132] There can be no doubt ungodliness has a direct impact on God!

Looking again at Ephesians 4:30, we recognize that the "grieving" of the Spirit would be caused by doing things that displease Him. This can be seen from the context of the verse. We've already read the verses leading up to it, so let us look at the verses which follow it.

Ephesians 4:30-32
And grieve not the holy Spirit of God, whereby ye are sealed unto the day of redemption. [31]Let all bitterness, and wrath, and anger, and clamour, and evil speaking, be put away from you, with all malice: [32]And be ye kind one to another, tenderhearted, forgiving one another, even as God for Christ's sake hath forgiven you.

God's Spirit is identified in a very unique way. Only one of God's attributes is used consistently throughout Scripture as the specific description of that Spirit. It is not the "Love Spirit" or the "Power Spirit" or the "Teaching Spirit" (although all of these things accompany the infilling of that Spirit). Rather, it is the "HOLY Spirit," indicating the most important reason why we must be filled with God's Spirit is to enable us to become holy!

---

[132] Barnes, A., J. G. Murphy, F. C. Cook, E. B. Pusey, H.C. Leupold, & R. Frew, *Barnes' Notes*. Blackie & Son, 1847.

> **1 Peter 1:15-16**
> *But as he which hath called you is holy, so be ye holy in all manner of conversation; ^{16}Because it is written, Be ye holy; for I am holy.*

The overarching will of God for our lives is that we take on His image – an image of holiness. This is explained in the Book of Romans.

> **Romans 8:28-29**
> *And we know that all things work together for good to them that love God, to them who are the called according to his purpose. ^{29}For whom he did foreknow, he also did predestinate to be conformed to the image of his Son, that he might be the firstborn among many brethren.*

Although verse 28 has been quoted often, I wonder how many people really understand what is being said. While the verse does say God will work things for our good, it says this happens for "them who are ... called according to HIS PURPOSE." The purpose of which Paul speaks is found in verse 29 when he writes that God's intention is for us to be "conformed to the image of His Son."

God allows difficult circumstances in our lives with the intent of ridding us of everything that is unlike Him. His goal and aim for us is to make us holy. When we allow ourselves to yield to worldly pleasures or dress in ungodly apparel, we are fighting against the will of God in our lives.

This would be a good time to address another common misconception. There are those who claim that since the New Testament Church is now "under grace," it means God simply does not hold us to account for our sin. Instead, they say, He overlooks it.

Such teaching is the furthest thing from the truth – and is, in fact, antithetical to the entire premise of Scripture! When Paul addressed the subject of us living under grace, he explicitly said it does NOT give us a license to continue to sin.

> **Romans 6:1-2**
> *What shall we say then? Shall we continue in sin, that grace may abound? ²God forbid. How shall we, that are dead to sin, live any longer therein?*

He then went on to say we should live free from sin. His reason was simple – it is BECAUSE we are under grace!

> **Romans 6:14**
> *For sin shall not have dominion over you: for ye are not under the law, but under grace.*

In his epistle to Titus, he explained grace in a way that is contrary to how it is presented in most churches today. According to Paul, grace is actually our instructor in righteousness!

> **Titus 2:11-12**
> *For the grace of God that bringeth salvation hath appeared to all men, ¹²Teaching us that, denying ungodliness and worldly lusts, we should live soberly, righteously, and godly, in this present world;*

Paul was not the only one to present this idea. The Apostle Jude also addressed grace from the same perspective.

> **Jude 1:4**
> *For there are certain men crept in unawares, who were before of old ordained to this condemnation, ungodly men, turning the grace of our God into lasciviousness, and denying the only Lord God, and our Lord Jesus Christ.*

When he said these "ungodly men" had turned grace into "lasciviousness," he was saying they were presenting God's grace as though it allowed us to live unrestrained lives of indulgent pleasure. That sounds a LOT like what many churches are doing today!

In his letter to Titus, Paul decried such an attitude. He wrote against those who make a profession of faith but do not live in accordance with God's Word.

Titus 1:16
They profess that they know God; but in works they deny him, being abominable, and disobedient, and unto every good work reprobate.

Grace is not a license to live as we please. Grace is God's strength granted to us so we can live pleasing unto Him!

Living a holy, separated life is not about obeying a list of rules in fear of punishment (whether from God or those in authority over us). It is about loving God so much we don't want to bring Him grief. We do not want to be involved in anything that would disappoint or sadden Him.

Because we don't want to frustrate God's grace or grieve His Spirit, there is an important consideration for us to ponder. It is based on a verse from the Book of Hebrews.

Hebrews 13:2
Be not forgetful to entertain strangers: for thereby some have entertained angels unawares.

When the apostle wrote these words, he addressed something far too many people overlook. There is a spiritual realm interacting directly with the physical realm in which we dwell.

The word "entertain," as it is used here, means to be hospitable towards someone or even to create a lodging for them. According to this verse, there are times when people have "entertained" angels (which this same epistle defines as "ministering spirits" in chapter 1, verse 14).

If angels are ministering spirits serving the saints, then

demons (fallen angels) are tormenting spirits trying the saints! Since it is possible to "entertain" the ministering spirits, it is also possible for some people to entertain the tormenting spirits!

I believe this is part of what is addressed in Ephesians. As Paul went through the list of ways we must behave to protect our spirit, he offered a specific directive involving the enemy.

Ephesians 4:27
Neither give place to the devil.

According to *Strong's Concordance,* the word "place" comes from the Greek word "topos," which means: "a place, a room, quarters ... any portion or space marked off ... from surrounding space; an inhabited place, as a city, village, or district."[133]

Several years ago, a highly respected man of God told the story of being awakened in the night and feeling the presence of Satan in his room. He tried rebuking the devil, but the evil spirit spoke to him and said, "I have permission to be here." He continued trying to rebuke the spirit but to no avail. Finally, he walked through the house and found a magazine someone had brought to his home that had demonic depictions in it. He burned it, rebuked the devil again, and this time got victory.

I believe there are things we can do, books we can read, places we can go, things we can watch, things we can listen to, and even attitudes we can develop, which create a "place" where the devil is "entertained" in our lives. Allowing ourselves to get involved in these things will "grieve" God's Holy Spirit!

Sadly, it seems much of what entertains the enemy is what sinners consider "entertainment" for themselves! For the church, it ought to be our desire to entertain ministering spirits rather than entertaining the spirits of Hell.

---

[133] Strong, James, *Strong's Exhaustive Concordance of the Bible,* Originally published 1890.

Grieve Not the Spirit

All of this leads me to wonder about something very troubling. Are we entertaining angelic spirits or being entertained by demons and the flesh?

With that question in mind, I will focus the remainder of this chapter on a few areas of entertainment of which we should be aware. In some cases, we should simply BEWARE altogether!

- Sports

One of the most common forms of entertainment today is sports. While I recognize this is a controversial subject, would you at least consider the following information?

Tom Brady (a famous quarterback) and some of his cohorts, developed a company (and website) called "The Religion of Sports." One of their founding statements says, "Sports aren't *like* religion. Sports *are* religion. They provide meaning, purpose, and significance to their participants—from athletes to spectators, coaches to broadcasters, family, friends, and fans. If sports are the faith, these are the faithful—and we are its disciples. Welcome to the Religion of Sports."[134] *[Emphasis added.]*

Many people are more faithful to their favorite sports team than they are to any church or religion. Sadly, many young people are much better at quoting sports statistics and players' positions than quoting Scriptures or identifying Biblical characters!

It is not difficult to compare a sports arena with a church, the exuberance of the fans with worship, and the adorning of a team's garb and/or colors with outward holiness standards. Doing so makes it easy to see that sports can be every bit as "demanding" as any religion.

Centuries ago, early church leaders preached against attending (or participating in) professional sporting events,

---

[134] Religion of Sports: Co-Founded by Tom Brady, Michael Strahan, and Gotham Chopra, as quoted by Elder Joe Savala in his article, *"Christianity and Sports,"* copyright JPS Ministries, 2021.

recognizing the atmosphere created by these events as totally contrary to everything Christians believed. For example, in his "Homilies Against Spectacles," John Chrysostom wrote, "It is evident that in Christian writings from the earliest centuries of the life of the Church, the attitude from the Fathers as to spectacles of [Greek confrontations] and Roman recreation expressly forbids attendance by Christians as spectators."[135] Until recently, this stand has remained consistent in most Apostolic churches.

The condemnation of involvement with professional sports was not historically limited to our movement. "Before the Civil War, clergymen and devoted lay people regarded sports as needless distractions and gateways to moral dissipation — clear competitors for sacred time and attention. A 17th-century English Puritan named Thomas Hall expressed a common view when he suggested that 'gaming' was among the surest means to 'debauch a people, and draw them from God and his worship to superstition and Idolatry.' 'We came into this world not for sport,' a Christian magazine opined in 1851, but 'for a higher and nobler object.' The fact that sports were often played on the Christian Sabbath made them all the more damnable. As the 20th century approached, however, attitudes toward sports pivoted."[136]

"Sports are succeeding by the measures that have traditionally defined success for religious institutions: regularly immersing people in a transcendent experience and keeping them ardently committed over the long term."[137]

Paul unequivocally stated that Christians are not to

---

[135] Chrysostom, John. *Homilies on the Epistle of St. Paul to the Ephesians. Homily 19.* In *The Nicene and Post-Nicene Fathers, First Series,* edited by Philip Schaff, Wm. B. Eerdmans Publishing Co., 1889.

[136] Washington Post, *Is Religion Losing Ground to Sports?*, https://www.washingtonpost.com/opinions/is-religion-losing-ground-to-sports/2014/01/31/6faa4d64-82bd-11e3-9dd4-e7278db80d86_story.html

[137] *Ibid.*

intermingle with ungodly practices. We are to have no fellowship with the works of darkness.

> ***1 Corinthians 10:20***
> *But I say, that the things which the Gentiles sacrifice, they sacrifice to devils, and not to God: and I would not that ye should have fellowship with devils.*

> ***2 Corinthians 6:14***
> *Be ye not unequally yoked together with unbelievers: for what fellowship hath righteousness with unrighteousness? and what communion hath light with darkness?*

When we attend, watch, or listen to a game, our hearts beat with the hearts of the other fans. Our cheers are lifted with theirs. We rejoice, get frustrated, and leave happy or disappointed – all in perfect concert with a stadium full of unbelievers. That sounds like "fellowship" to me!

- Technology

Another area of concern involves current technology – especially things offered via the internet. More specifically, social media has captured the attention – and abundant participation – of millions.

While I will not take the time to outline all the obvious dangers of these sites (nor name them specifically), I do think it behooves us as Christians to recognize the pitfalls of joining such sites. Something about "hiding" behind a screen seems to cause many to lose all caution and abandon all filters when addressing others. Far too often, "dirty laundry" is aired for the public, personal vendettas are launched, vengeance is sought, and attacks are made in which Christians should never participate.

There have even been those who dare to argue various points of "holiness" in front of hundreds of sinners with whom they are connected in the medium of their choice (Facebook, Twitter/X, etc.). What kind of impression does that make on unbelievers as they watch Christians argue over some difference in our personal standards?

Another problem with these forms of media is the inordinate amount of time that is wasted. Hundreds of hours pass while viewing "reels," "shorts," "clips," and sometimes even movies on Instagram, YouTube, and other venues – all while condemning the watching of television and going to theaters! This is NOT to condone the latter, but rather to show the inconsistency in which it is all too easy to find ourselves.

The people of God should not be guilty of wasting vast portions of our precious time on trivial activities with no benefit to us or anyone else. Especially in these last days, we should REDEEM the time, NOT waste it!

Ephesians 5:16
Redeeming the time, because the days are evil.

"Redeeming" means "to buy up for oneself, for one's use ... the meaning seems to be to make a wise and sacred use of every opportunity for doing good, so that zeal and well-doing are as it were the purchase-money by which we make the time our own."[138]

Besides being a waste of time, there are other dangers associated with various kinds of technology. Many of today's electronic games offer "chat" options. Tragically, perverted people take advantage of these chats to lure unsuspecting children into horrific situations.

One highly popular video game recently came under fire after adding a new feature. Players would enter a room and find a demonic creature seated on a throne. They would then be offered a chilling option – to sell their soul in exchange for benefits within

---

[138] Thayer, J., *A Greek-English Lexicon of the New Testament,* Baker Book House, 1993.

the game.[139]

Playing games involving violent and/or other criminal activities is certainly not spiritually healthy. This is especially true if the activity is among those things God considers an abomination (such as murder). Once again, let me stress we should not even bring an abomination into our homes. (See Deuteronomy 7:26.)

Artificial Intelligence ("AI") is also presenting a problem. Socialist James Haidt says, "The mass migration of childhood into the virtual world has disrupted social and neurological development. This disruption includes social anxiety, sleep deprivation, attention fragmentation, and addiction."[140] Consequentially, one 14-year-old took his life because he "fell in love" with an AI-generated character that encouraged him to do so.[141]

At the time of this writing, YouTube is extremely popular, even among many Apostolics. While the following statistics do not focus on Apostolic homes, they are staggering nonetheless. "Fully 80% of all parents with a child age 11 or younger say their child [sometimes] watches videos on YouTube, with 53% reporting that their child does this daily, including about a third who say this happens several times a day (35%)."[142]

---

[139] Express Tribune, *Fortnite Faces Backlash Over New Feature Allowing Players to "Sell Their Soul" to Revive Teammates,* https://tribune.com.pk/story/2502902/fortnite-faces-backlash-over-new-feature-allowing-players-to-sell-their-soul-to-revive-teammates, October 15, 2024.

[140] Haidt, Jonathan, The Anxious Generation, https://www.anxiousgeneration.com, Accessed March 13, 2025.

[141] The Independent, *The Disturbing Messages Between AI Chatbot and Teen Who Took His Own Life,* https://www.the-independent.com/news/world/americas/crime/ai-chatbot-lawsuit-sewell-setzer-b2635090.html, October 24, 2024.

[142] Pew Research Center, *Parental Views About YouTube,* https://www.pewresearch.org/internet/2020/07/28/parental-views-about-youtube, July 28, 2020.

"YouTube [is] no place for kids — of any age — to roam alone," according to cyber education consultant Lori Getz.[143] One doctor said, "A child has the ability to jump from a harmless video, for example, about birds, to a video with adult content, all within a matter of seconds."[144]

Dr. Brandon Smith, assistant professor of pediatrics at Johns Hopkins in Baltimore, has addressed other concerns. "Studies in preschoolers have shown a relationship between poor impulse control and self-regulation with earlier and longer use of low-quality media. It's also thought that excessive screen time with low-quality media may contribute to poorer language development in certain children."[145]

One final area of warning that I feel I must offer is the danger of allowing the internet to provide too many voices in our lives. Paul wrote about "many voices," stating they all have some significance (1 Corinthians 14:10). Earlier in his letter, however, he made it clear that his voice ought to be the most important.

1 Corinthians 4:15-16
For though ye have ten thousand instructors in Christ, yet have ye not many fathers: for in Christ Jesus I have begotten you through the gospel.
[16]Wherefore I beseech you, be ye followers of me.

There are many options available via the internet today. Podcasts and church service streams are plenteous. My concern is that when these options start bringing confusion by presenting ideas contrary to what is taught in the local church.

Even if the source to which you are listening is Apostolic, you should always let your pastor's voice be the "loudest,"

---

[143] Care.com, *9 Red Flags of YouTube for Kids and Tips for Safer Viewing*, https://www.care.com/c/how-youtube-affects-kids
[144] *Ibid.*
[145] *Ibid.*

strongest, and most influential in your life. He is the watchman God has placed in your life, and no one should take his place.

Another problem is when a member of one church begins listening to (or perhaps even watching) the services of an assembly that is not their home church. It may become a temptation to compare standards – or supposed "benefits" (*i.e.,* what the other church has to offer) – and decide to change churches based on what they hear or see.

God placed you in your church for a reason. While there are times when a transfer is necessary, it should not be done for selfish reasons – and never without the godly counsel of your pastor!

When I opened this chapter, I dealt with the fact that it is impossible for me to cover every issue connected to holiness and separation. Nevertheless, I have tried to supply enough principles to provide guidance in most areas. One day, I may update this book to address additional topics, especially as the world changes and other challenges arise. The main thing to keep in mind is we must become more diligent than ever before in guarding our spirit, soul, and body!

The entire point of this chapter – and this book – is that WHATEVER we do or allow should NEVER "grieve" the Holy Spirit of God. In fact, let us look at our opening verse again.

> ***Ephesians 4:30***
> *And grieve not the holy Spirit of God, whereby ye are sealed unto the day of redemption.*

There is another way to think about "grieving" the Holy Ghost. You see, the Holy Ghost is associated with fire.

> ***Luke 3:16***
> *John answered, saying unto them all, I indeed baptize you with water; but one mightier than I cometh, the latchet of whose shoes I am not worthy to unloose: he shall baptize you with the Holy Ghost and with fire:*

There are two ways to extinguish a fire. You can grieve it or quench it. Interestingly, both of these terms are used to describe the treatment of the Spirit of God in our lives.

1 Thessalonians 5:19
Quench not the Spirit.

To "quench" a fire, one must add adverse materials (water, dirt, chemicals, etc.) that cover the flames completely. Contrary to the way this verse is often used, the actual idea behind Paul's admonition not to "quench" the Holy Ghost has NOTHING to do with worship and EVERYTHING to do with lifestyle!

To "grieve" a fire, one must remove from it all that is flammable – such as digging a trench around it or removing the oxygen (*i.e.,* covering a candle in a glass container) and thereby "smothering" it. Paul admonished us not to "grieve" the Holy Ghost – thus, we must be careful not to "smother" the Spirit of God within us by surrounding ourselves with things that are not conducive to the working of that Spirit in accordance with His will for our lives!

Our goal is to keep the fire burning. To do so, we must continually present ourselves as a living sacrifice (see Romans 12:1). God's Spirit can empower us to overcome the sinful desires of the flesh. (See Galatians 5:16.)

Ephesians 3:16
That he would grant you, according to the riches of his glory, to be strengthened with might by his Spirit in the inner man;

The strength of God's Spirit will enable us to live a holy life. A consistent practice of praying in the Spirit (see Romans 8:23-26), church attendance (see Hebrews 10:26), and Bible reading (see Psalm 119:11) will provide protection, guidance, insight, and Spiritual nourishment. The end result will be a lifestyle of separation – from the world and unto God!

BIBLIOGRAPHY

American Addiction Centers, *The Link Between Child Abuse and Substance Abuse,* https://americanaddictioncenters.org/blog/the-link-between-child-abuse-and-substance-abuse, Updated April 30, 2024.

American Cancer Society, *Why People Start Smoking and Why its Hard to Stop,* https://www.cancer.org/cancer/risk-prevention/tobacco/guide-quitting-smoking/why-people-start-using-tobacco.html, Accessed March 12, 2025.

American Heart Association, *What You Need to Know about Vaping,* https://www.heart.org/en/health-topics/house-calls/what-you-need-to-know-about-vaping, Accessed March 12, 2025.

BAKER, W., & E. E. Carpenter, *The Complete Word Study Dictionary: Old Testament,* AMG Publishers. 2003.

BARNES, A., J.G. Murphy, F.C. Cook, E.B. Pusey, H.C. Leupold, & R. Frew, *Barnes' Notes*. Blackie & Son, 1847.

BERNARD, David K., *Practical Holiness: A Second Look,* Word Aflame Press, 1985.

BROWN, Francis, Samuel Rolles Driver, and Charles Augustus Briggs. *A Hebrew and English Lexicon of the Old Testament.* Houghton Mifflin Company, 1906.

Care.com, *9 Red Flags of YouTube for Kids and Tips for Safer Viewing,* https://www.care.com/c/how-youtube-affects-kids, October 20, 2022.

CBS News, *50% of Doctors Prescribe Placebos,* https://www.cbsnews.com/news/50-of-doctors-prescribe-placebos, October 24, 2008.

Centers for Disease Control, *Facts About U.S. Deaths from Excessive Alcohol Use,* https://www.cdc.gov/alcohol/facts-stats/index.html, August 6, 2024.

Centers for Disease Control, *Impaired Driving,* https://www.cdc.gov/impaired-driving/facts/index.html, May 16, 2024.

Bibliography

Centers for Disease Control, *Smoking and Tobacco Use*, https://www.cdc.gov/tobacco/e-cigarettes/about.html, October 24, 2024.

Christianity.com, *What is the Sin of Gluttony, and What are its Consequences?*, https://www.christianity.com/wiki/sin/what-is-the-sin-of-gluttony-its-definition-and-consequences.html, Updated May 22, 2024.

CHRYSOSTOM, John. *Homilies on the Epistle of St. Paul to the Ephesians. Homily 19.* In *The Nicene and Post-Nicene Fathers, First Series,* edited by Philip Schaff, Wm. B. Eerdmans Publishing Co., 1889.

CLARKE, Adam. *Adam Clarke's Commentary on the Bible.* Originally published 1810–1826.

Cleveland Clinic, *Second Hand Smoke,* https://my.clevelandclinic.org/health/articles/10644-secondhand-smoke-dangers, Accessed March 12, 2025.

CONLON, Michael, Reuters, *TV and Other Factors Lead to Early Teen Sex: Study,* https://www.reuters.com/article/lifestyle/tv-and-other-factors-lead-to-early-teen-sex-study-idUSTRE4AO049, November 24, 2008.

CVETKOVSKA, Ljubica, Modern Gentleman, *26 Beard Statistics and Facts You Probably Didn't Know,* https://moderngentlemen.net/beard-statistics, January 1, 2021.

CYPRIAN, Saint, Eternal World Television Network, *The Dress of Virgins,* https://www.ewtn.com/catholicism/library/dress-of-virgins-12507, Accessed March 13, 2025.

Decibel Pro, *Rock Concert Decibels Estimated,* https://decibelpro.app/blog/how-loud-is-a-rock-concert, Accessed March 13, 2025.

Dictionary.com, www.dictionary.com, Accessed March 12, 2025.

Douay-Rheims Bible, Loreto Publications, 2020.

DUPONT, Laurent, Research Gate, https://www.researchgate.net/figure/Edgar-Dale-Audio-Visual-Methods-in-Teaching-3rd-Edition-Holt-Rinehart-and-Winston_fig1_283011989, June 2013.

EMERSON, Ralph Waldo, *Sow a Thought and You Reap an Action, The Complete Works of Ralph Waldo Emerson,* edited by Edward Waldo Emerson, vol. 2, Houghton, Mifflin and Company, 1883.

Express Tribune, *Fortnite Faces Backlash Over New Feature Allowing Players to 'Sell Their Soul' to Revive Teammates,* https://tribune.com.pk/story/2502902/fortnite-faces-backlash-over-new-feature-allowing-players-to-sell-their-soul-to-revive-teammates, October 15, 2024.

GARNER, Tom, Live Science, https://www.livescience.com/iwo-jima-flag-raising.html, February 23, 2021.

God's Word Translation, Baker Books, 2010.

Golden Book Magazine, Volume 14, Published by The Review of Reviews Corporation, Albert Shaw, New York. 1931.

GORE, Chancy, *Facial Hair - A Christian Perspective,* Advance Ministries, 1998.

GRIFFIN, Kelsey, Dan Segraves, Ralph Reynold, Rick Wyser, *Why? A Study of Christian Standards,* Word Aflame Publications. 1984.

GUZIK, David. Study Guide for James 3, *Warnings and Words to Teachers*, Blue Letter Bible, 2018. https://www.blueletterbible.org/comm/guzik_david/study-guide/james/james-3.cfm, Accessed March 13, 2025.

HAIDT, Jonathan, The Anxious Generation, https://www.anxiousgeneration.com, Accessed March 13, 2025.

HARLEY, Dr. Willard F., Jr., *His Needs, Her Needs,* Baker Publishing Group, 2011.

Bibliography

HENRY, M., *Matthew Henry's Commentary on the Whole Bible*, Fleming H. Revell, 1935.

Holman Christian Standard Bible, Holman Bible Publishers, 2004.

HOOKE, S. H., *The Bible in Basic English*, Cambridge University Press, 1982.

JAMIESON, Robert, Andrew Robert Fausset, and David Brown, *Commentary on the Whole Bible*. Originally published 1871.

Johns Hopkins Medicine, *5 Vaping Facts You Need to Know*, https://www.hopkinsmedicine.org/health/wellness-and-prevention/5-truths-you-need-to-know-about-vaping, Accessed March 12, 2025.

Johns Hopkins Medicine, *Smoking and Respiratory Diseases*, https://www.hopkinsmedicine.org/health/conditions-and-diseases/smoking-and-respiratory-diseases, Accessed March 12, 2025.

LEGON, Jeordan, CNN, *From Science and Computers, a New Face of Jesus*, https://www.cnn.com/2002/TECH/science/12/25/face.jesus/index.html, December 26, 2002.

MALINS, Joseph, *A Fence or an Ambulance*, 1895 or 1898 (sources uncertain), printed in the Iowa Health Bulletin in 1912.

Merriam-Webster Dictionary, https://www.merriam-webster.com/dictionary, Accessed March 12, 2025.

Mill, John Stuart, *System of Logic*, Baptist Missionary Press, 1821.

MITCHELL, Ben, *The Works of the Flesh (Galatians 5:19)*, published by the Christian Life Commission of the Southern Baptist Convention, Nashville, TN [date unknown].

National Highway Safety Administration, *Drunk Driving*, https://www.nhtsa.gov/risky-driving/drunk-driving, Accessed March 12, 2025.

NeuroLaunch, *Music's Negative Effects on the Brain: Exploring the Dark Side of Melodies,* https://neurolaunch.com/how-music-affects-the-brain-negatively, Updated October 2, 2024.

Northwestern Medicine, https://www.nm.org/healthbeat/healthy-tips/alcohol-and-the-brain, Updated November 2023.

Online Etymology Dictionary, https://www.etymonline.com, Accessed March 12, 2025.

OULLETTE, Dr. R. B., Ministry 127, https://ministry127.com/christian-living/keeping-your-spirit-right, May 13, 2020.

PATTON, William, *The Laws of Fermentation and the Wines of the Ancients,* National Temperance Society and Publication House, 1872.

PAULOSE, Dr. K.O., *Gluttony – Is it a Sin?,* https://drpaulose.com/spirituality/gluttony-is-it-a-sin, May 5, 2008.

PAYNE, Leah, *"God Gave Rock & Roll to You: a history of contemporary Christian music",* Oxford University Press, 2024.

PETERKIN, Alan, *One Thousand Beards: A Cultural History of Facial Hair,* Arsenal Pulp Press, 2001.

Peterson, Eugene, *The Message Bible,* Playaway Publishers, 2010.

Pew Research Center, *Parental Views About YouTube,* https://www.pewresearch.org/internet/2020/07/28/parental-views-about-youtube, July 28, 2020.

Public Broadcasting System, *The History of the American Flag,* https://www.pbs.org/a-capitol-fourth/history/old-glory, Accessed March 12, 2025.

Religion of Sports: Co-Founded by Tom Brady, Michael Strahan, and Gotham Chopra, as quoted by Elder Joe Savala in his article, *"Christianity and Sports,"* copyright JPS Ministries, 2021.

Bibliography

RICHARDS, Louisa, and Cynthia Taylor Chavoustie, MPAS, PA-C, Medical News Today, https://www.medicalnewstoday.com/articles/how-many-drinks-does-it-take-to-get-drunk, Updated September 26, 2023.

RIGGEN, Gregory, *The Madness and Method of Modern Music,* New Life Ministries, 1988.

RIGGEN, Gregory, *Understanding the Godhead,* New Life Ministries, 2019.

RIGGEN, Gregory, *Understanding the New Birth,* New Life Ministries, 2019.

SCHRECKENBERG, G. M., & Bird, H. H. *Neural Plasticity of Mus Musculus in Response to Disharmonic Sound.* The Bulletin of the New Jersey Academy of Science, 1987.

SPENCE-JONES, Henry Donald Maurice, and Joseph S. Exell, editors, *The Pulpit Commentary,* Funk & Wagnalls Company, 1890–1919.

STEWART, Missionary Jessie, *Inward Holiness,* taught at a conference in the Republic of South Africa on March 28, 2024.

STRONG, James, *Strong's Exhaustive Concordance of the Bible,* Originally published 1890.

THAYER, J., *A Greek-English Lexicon of the New Testament,* Baker Book House, 1993.

The Ante-Nicene Fathers, Volume IV. Alexander Roberts and James Donaldson, editors. W.B. Eerdmans Pub. Co, 1973.

The Holy Bible: The Common English Bible, Abingdon Press, 2011.

The Contemporary English Version, Thomas Nelson Publishers, 1995.

The Holy Bible: Darby Translation; Christian Classics Ethereal Library; 2002.

The Holy Bible: English Standard Version, Crossway Books, 2001.

The Holy Bible: International Standard Version, Davidson Press, 2003.

The Holy Bible: New Century Version, Thomas Nelson Publishers, 1991.

The Holy Bible: New International Reader's Version, Zondervan, 2016.

The Independent, *The Disturbing Messages Between AI Chatbot and Teen Who Took His Own Life,* https://www.theindependent.com/news/world/americas/crime/ai-chatbot-lawsuit-sewell-setzer-b2635090.html, October 24, 2024.

The New King James Bible, Worldwide Publishers, 2017.

VINE, W.E., J.R. Kohlenberger, J.A. Swanson, *The Expanded Vine's Expository Dictionary of New Testament Words.* Bethany House Publishers, 1984.

Washington Post, *Is Religion Losing Ground to Sports?,* https://www.washingtonpost.com/opinions/is-religion-losing-ground-to-sports/2014/01/31/6faa4d64-82bd-11e3-9dd4-e7278db80d86_story.html, January 31, 2014.

WILKERSON, David, *Set the Trumpet to Thy Mouth,* Sovereign World Publishers, 1985.

Wordnik.com, https://www.wordnik.com/words/dissipate, Accessed March 12, 2025.

World English Bible, Librivox, 2017.

ABOUT THE AUTHOR

Pastor Gregory K. Riggen was born in 1960 to (at that time) non-Christian parents, He began attending an Apostolic Pentecostal Church at the age of 11. The following year, He received the Holy Ghost and was baptized in Jesus' name. He subsequently led his entire family to the Lord. He felt a call into the ministry that summer, and preached his first message on a Wednesday night at the age of 13.

Pastor Riggen received his Th.B. from Texas Bible College in Houston. With a 4.0 average, he was valedictorian of his graduating class. He entered into full-time ministry immediately upon graduation.

At the age of 24, he accepted his first pastorate. He has pastored in Texas, Colorado, Mississippi, and Kansas.

In 1988, Pastor Riggen published his first book, "The Madness and Method of Modern Music." He has written numerous articles, as well as several lessons for Word Aflame Publications. He has also written and published two Home Bible Studies.

In 2013, Pastor Riggen was invited to Zimbabwe to address a number of Trinitarian Pentecostal pastors. That meeting resulted in more than 50 pastors and wives being baptized in Jesus' name. As a result, he founded A2Z Missions, which has since gone into the countries of Botswana, Malawi, South Africa, Swaziland, and Zambia. Literally hundreds of pastors have received the revelation of the Mighty God in Christ and have been baptized in the name of Jesus because of the teaching they received at his conferences.

Pastor Riggen has pastored the Truth Church in Olathe, Kansas for almost 30 years. During this time, he has been instrumental in the planting of three "daughter works.". His vision is to plant many more churches throughout the greater Kansas City metropolitan area while continuing to oversee the work in Olathe.

He and his wife, Rhonda (Yates) Riggen, have been married 45 years. They have three children and ten grandchildren.

www.ingramcontent.com/pod-product-compliance
Lightning Source LLC
Chambersburg PA
CBHW052135070526
44585CB00017B/1834